VISION

The search for ways to increase sexual desire and boost the libido is as old as humanity itself, and the connection between nourishment of the body and nourishment of the senses has always been a close one. The celebrated womaniser, Giacoma Cassanova took it to be his natural right to share more than a meal with his female dining companions - diner à deux is today what it always has been - lustful temptation.

In Europe - and all over the world - there is a close and traditional connection between taste, smells and intense longing, which is at times welcomed, and at others is socially unacceptable. In Asia, the sensual and spiritual Hindu and Buddhist practise of Tantra blends culinary and sexual eroticism in order to bring the essential life energies to awareness. 'The Erotic Cookbook' is a feast for the senses, exploring the realms of appetite and the enjoyment of indulgence.

Cristina Moles Kaupp studied German, Political Science and Journalism. She has worked for the past ten years as a journalist for, among other publications, the Berlin town magazine 'Tip', the 'Tagesspiegel' and the 'Sender Freies Berlin'.

# The
# Erotic Cookbook

*Cristina Moles Kaupp*

**English edition and translation: Sheena Dewan**

First published in Great Britain in 1999 by VISION Paperbacks, a division of Satin Publications Limited.



VISION Paperbacks,
a division of
Satin Publications Limited
20 Queen Anne Street
London W1M 0AY
E-mail: sheenadewan@compuserve.com

Design and layout: Justine Hounam

Additional translating: Angela Hounam and Liz Clark
Printed and bound by:
Caledonian International Book Manufacturing
Internal illustrations: Thomas August Günther


ISBN: 1-901250-33-4

# CONTENTS

## THE WAY TO A MAN'S HEART IS THROUGH HIS STOMACH

*The man loves white; his shirt, vest, trousers - even his hat is snow white. He is almost like a dandy in a book - one who has taste as well as a love of life. His wife suits him - she is pure luxury; young, graceful, playful and always smiling. Now, she is lying naked in the hotel bed, half covered by a lightly-coloured sheet. She is watched by him, as he stands in the middle of the room, thoughtfully pouring champagne into a tall fluted glass.*

*There is a knock. The hotel boy brings in fresh supplies, while staring with embarrassment at the woman's naked breast. Even more champagne, crustaceans and other delicacies? The man lifts his glass, and she winks at him, finally saying 'come to me' with her eyes. A kiss. Tender nibbling of the earlobe. His tongue licks her smooth armpit as he reaches for the salt cellar. Slowly, he trickles salt over her nipple, and stretches for half the lemon, which smiles at him from the fruit bowl. Squeezes it over her breast. He sucks greedily - salt, lemon, pips, everything. She moans and turns to crawl over him and to the pot of cream. She dips her breast into it and moves back to him. Stuffs his throat full of warm flesh and soft white, which he loves so much. Lies next to him, fingers in front of mouth. Is that honey which suddenly, slowly drips down? It is simply licked up. Now a sip of red wine. He pours it into a glass bowl, and grabs a small shrimp, still alive, and throws it into the wine. He pours it quickly over his beauty's stomach. A panicking animal tickles her beautiful abdomen in the throes of drunken death.*

Scene from the Japanese Film 'Tampopo, or the Secret of Noodle Soup' by Juzo Itami.

*He stands at the sea and observes a young female oyster farmer emerging from the waves. Her pale dress clings to her slight figure. Dripping, she stands before him.*
*'What did you get out of the sea?' he asks.*
*She shows him her basket of oysters.*

*'May I have one?'*

*She nods, opens one up and offers him the shimmering shell. He takes it and presses it passionately against his mouth. He pulls back suddenly - lip bleeding. Regretfully, he lowers the shell and stares at the girl.*

*'Can I help you?' She takes the shell and cuts out the flesh - it slips into her wet hand. Searching glances, a drop of blood falls onto the shining oyster flesh. Hastily he gulps it down. He stays, anticipating the aftertaste. So beautifully white, wild black hair, the fresh red on his lips. She can't resist. She reaches up to him and licks his blood in lust.*

Scene from the Japanese Film 'Tampopo, or the Secret of Noodle Soup' by Juzo Itami.

Many theories have been based on the premise that the search for food comes over and above the desire to mate and reproduce, and that nature places hunger before sexuality.

The eating of one's sexual partner may seem unimaginable, but it is quite common for a number of single-cell organisms, as well as some spiders and insects. This practise may lie at the 'dubious' end of the moral scale, but it could possibly also indicate the beginnings of sexuality.

Various scientific theories and many sayings such as 'I love you so much I could eat you up' show the close connection between eating and eroticism, and even religions make an issue of this. For example, Catholicism teaches the doctrine of transubstantiation, that being the mystical process of the communion bread and wine becoming Christ's body and blood when it is taken at the altar. Christ said 'Take this bread and eat this for it is my body. Take this wine and drink it, for it is my blood.'

The rite of communion not only goes back to the ancient custom of human sacrifice, but also to the belief that the energy and essence of the devoured person is somehow absorbed by the eater, and as a result, one gets as close as possible to them. Who can doubt that the celebration of communion contains erotic references - that of the ecstatic desire for unity?

Artemisia ground up the bones of her husband after he died, and drank the powder in scented water, as she considered there was no better place than her body to keep her loved one. Many other myths, fairy tales and significant works of literature show a close connection between cannibalism and eroticism, such as 'Penthesilea' by Heinrich von Kleist, 'Ulysses' by James Joyce or '120 Days of Sodom' from the Marquis de Sade.

Adam and Eve encountered eroticism for the first time when they stole the forbidden apple and exposed their inner selves, their curiosity and readiness to break the rules. They provoked the final separation of the table and the bed, and so instilled in our hearts the longing for the unity of one with the other. That eroticism and food share a bed, that hunger not only means a longing for food but also sex, has since become universally understood.

## TREATING A 'CRAZY' CONDITION

The longing for arousal is in many ways a 'crazy' condition, in that it has no bearing on the survival of the organism or the perpetuation of the species in a direct way. And yet, humans are obsessed by the pursuit of the fulfilment of erotic desire. Through the ages, there is barely a herb or animal that has not been used in an elixir or potion in the attempt to increase sexual appetite; creams, amulets, magic spells - they have all been tried.

The survival instincts of animals seem to be far more honed

than that of humans; they are stronger, braver, faster and more fertile. And, they are not distracted by the paradoxes and complexities of sexual gratification. Animals often have sharper senses and frightening and effective weapons at their disposal, without having to resort to tools: horns, claws, poisons, teeth and in some cases even electric shocks and offensive odours.

There is also the frequency of their mating, and in many cases, the relative size of their sexual organs. Humans have been long impressed by this and as a result have ascribed unique powers of potency and virility to animals. In many myths, the gods disguised themselves as animals: Zeus came to earth as a bull on one occasion, and on another, he transformed himself into a horse in order to mate with a nymph who had changed herself into a mare to escape his advances. In other cultures, there is an enduring fear of the power of animals, both real and mythical; the Germane feared the werewolf, and in the Congo, the legend of leopard-men is still alive.

There is no pharmacological evidence to suggest that animal -based aphrodisiacs increase sexual desire, and yet to this day, animal horns, testicles and bones are held in high esteem, sometimes causing species to become endangered, or even extinct. He who wears an amulet made of the chosen body part, grinds antlers, bull or rhinoceros horn into a love potion, or even eats dried testicles and penises, hopes that the sexual desire and strength of the creature will be passed on to him.

An oil-beetle, known in ancient times as Cantharis (now confusingly known as the 'Spanish fly') is one of the most popular aphrodisiacs. It contains the poisonous substance Cantharidin, and is said to guarantee, when powdered and used in small doses, a huge increase in sex drive. Despite its dangerous side effects - as little as 30mg can be fatal - this green beetle ends up in numerous love potions and creams.

Plants must also hold aphrodisiacal powers, on the grounds

that they possess such a vibrant array of colours, forms and scents, not to mention poisons. As with the animal kingdom, plants were also imbued with the qualities and personalities of the gods. Zeus lived in the oak tree, and Athena in the olive tree. Pan was embodied in ivy, Wotan in the ash and Hathor, the Egyptian mother of all gods in the fig tree. The trunk, bark, leaves and the fruit of these and other plants were therefore filled with godly strength and qualities. The roots of these holy plants, bearing deep into the earth were considered to be conduits for vital earth energy.

This energy is believed to be expressed in the scent and aroma of the plant. The burning of leaves, stems, flowers and resins of plants is, in many cultures believed to help free the soul from the body and bring the individual nearer to the realm of the gods. Special, secret scents have been passed down from as far back as the ancient Egyptians. In India, bewitching smoke, and the spraying of aphrodisiac essences such as sandalwood, cinnamon oil or musk, were part of the sexual rituals of the practitioners of Tantra.

Today, manufactured perfumes are more widely used than natural scents, and their ingredients are both plant and animal derived. The most commonly used animal derivatives are glandular secretions, which are produced by the animal while they are on heat or during the breeding season. Castoreum, musk and zibet are all harvested from animals, sometimes with considerable cruelty involved. Nevertheless, most humans find these aromas breathtaking.

In the 1960s and 70s, incense was a common accompaniment to sexual discovery and experimentation, and nowadays there is further interest in a return to natural scents, with the increasing popularity of aromatherapy oils and the atmospheric moods they evoke.

## SYMPATHY

With the knowledge of lust, man was finally driven from paradise. On the path of evolution, the 'centre' of the body shifted away from the loins and moved to the head. Intuitions were forgotten and moral questions regarding good and bad was answered rationally rather than unconsciously. There was no going back.

Nevertheless, nature itself continued to provide helpful hints, which man had no choice but to learn and respect. Behind the wealth of substances, colours, forms and smells, humans would always suspect that there were hidden codes shrouded in the natural world. If they could be deciphered, perhaps the mysterious relationship between minerals, plants, animals and humans could be revealed.

At least, this was the view of doctor, Philippus Aureoles Theophrastes von Hohenheim, also known by the name of Paracelsus. He pioneered a new form of medicine in the 16th century, through which medical knowledge was gleaned purely from observation of nature - 'the corpus (body) and its purpose is one thing'. He believed very star, every body, every material, element and organ possesses specific qualities, which attracted or repelled. Sympathy or antipathy, relationships or enmities, these polarities and signs of nature and the stars needed to be explained. This view played a big role in the Middle Ages, not only in explaining the world, but also in the preparation of medicines and aphrodisiacs.

In those days, sexuality had a relatively free reign in Europe, against which, at the beginning at least, the church fought a losing battle. In fact, unintentionally, the Church encouraged free sexuality, because the crusade brought public baths to Central Europe from which brothels later sprung forth. In these public baths everything possible was done to create an erotic atmosphere;

they burnt seeds and leaves of the henbane plant and served stimulating food and drinks.

Ultimately, as a result of increasing political pressure, the church gained ground in its fight to end such liberties. They proclaimed that everything that seemed immodest was prohibited; anything sexual, which was not directly concerned with procreation was unacceptable. Highly spiced food and roasted meat were on the index of forbidden foods. As a diet against wantonness, dishes were served which kept 'the body damp and cold, for instance pumpkins, melons, acetic acid and bitter food, boiled lentils seasoned with vinegar' (from Francesco Rappi: 'New Little Treasure Trove, the three chastities.'in Piero Campresi's 'The Secrets of Venus'). The strongest permitted aid for stimulation between married couples was a milky vegetable soup with fresh bread and half-cooked egg white, which was supposed to raise the level of potency in a man to ensure a happy marriage.

But limits were even laid down for sex within marriage. Intercourse was only allowed in one position. Other, 'indecent' variations, were punished with seven years in jail. Coitus was forbidden altogether on certain days: Sundays, Wednesdays and Fridays; forty days before Easter and Christmas; up to forty days after birth and three days before communion - at which regular attendance was required, and the confession beforehand acted as a perfect instrument to check on observance.

However, the coitus of food and sex continued. It was not by chance that in the Middle Ages an erotic lovers' meal took place in the bathroom next to the bedroom. And it was not only Giacomo Casanova who regarded it as his right, after a meal, to unite his body with that of his table-companion, as described in his 'History of my Life'.

In order to survive the 'war on sex', many sought advice and support from wise women, witches, alchemists and doctors. These, ironically, relied on recipes put together from Godly inspirations and earlier Church texts. Plants which resembled the human sex-organs or whose juice smelt like sperm or vaginal secretion, were thought to stimulate one's love life. Asparagus, root vegetables, cucumber, morel and certain roots simply had to be good for the man's penis; things which resembled the vagina - apricots, plums, peaches - could only kindle the flame of a woman.

The search for effective herbs for love-potions continued - the devil's and witches' work in some people's view, a gift from heaven for others. But the church did not sleep. Monks were asked to research herbs, which would dampen sexual desire or kill it altogether. The monk's tree, water-lily and the so-called monks' pepper had the reputation of dampening longing, but these plants fortunately did not have the desired effect on society.

The wise women and their secrets were always one step ahead. They knew of tinctures that ostensibly reduced the size of breasts and made them firm, methods which made 'worn-out' women younger, or to make those who had lost their virginity virgins once more. They knew of magic which could guarantee the love of a particular person or which could tame obstinate people. But their most famous mixture was what was known as 'enticing cream'. The exact content of this narcotic and psychedelic mixture has not been passed down. Fats, incense, seasoning, certain poisons and aphrodisiacs were some of the ingredients. Witch-hunters suspected it contained human-fat and boiled babies bodies, sleeping oil, dragon's blood and devil's dirt!

In the Middle Ages and the Renaissance, alchemists and the Sympathy Cult returned to using roots again. They were also interested in human organs, using Paracelsus' theory: 'The most effective medicine for humans is man'. This was also the opinion of the Italian astrologer and doctor Girolamo Manfredi who said: 'There is no thing or food which would be more acceptable as nourishment for humans than human flesh, if nature didn't make it so repulsive'.

The witches' superstitions involved using parts of the human body for some of their medicines: the heart, eyes, sexual organs, liver and kidneys. As recently as the 19th century, the body parts of executed people were considered to contain magical powers. In ancient times the liver was thought to be the seat of the soul and was supposed to be the repository of wisdom and sexual energy. Penises and fingers sold very well as 'thieves candles'. The fat from poor sinners and babies' blood was added to an assortment of creams designed to guard against impotence.

In early modern times, Egyptian mummies were brought to Europe. They were turned into tinctures by apothecaries and had a reputation of being a cure-all and aphrodisiac. The pharmacist E. Merk from Darmstadt in Germany offered them in his catalogue 'Mumia vera aegyptica' for 17.50 marks per kilo. Among other things, mother's milk, ear wax, urine or excrement, secretion from the foreskin glands or sperm were prescribed. Those who find this revolting and are glad not to have lived in those times should remember that some beauty creams, even today, contain parts of placentas.

Probably some of the 'barbaric' methods had high therapeutic value. In recent years, ancient therapies such as urine therapy have enjoyed a comeback.

## THE KAMA SUTRA

That there are less drastic ways to assist ones love life, can be seen in the teachings about love in the East. The Kama Sutra taught that sexual satisfaction is of particular importance for the well-being of both men and women. This view was damned in Europe by the Church until this century. Women had, according to the Christian Church, no right to their own sexuality, let alone a satisfying one. In the Kama Sutra, sexual partners were categorised and matched according to the size of their sexual organs: men in buck, bull and stallion, the women in gazelle, mare and elephant-cow. For sexual intercourse, the love-book has 64 positions, which are poetically described in detail. Sado-masochistic practices and the use of dildos were integrated into sex games, as well as male homosexuality. However, interestingly lesbianism was not permitted. The Kama Sutra also recommended recipes for love-potions, cosmetics, medicine and magic.

The Tantrists passed on many rituals and recipes for increasing sexual pleasure and psychic powers. Students of tantra learn the details about sexual behaviour, which are often not understood in the Western culture and considered pornography. Yet their rituals serve to blend yin and yang to their original unity. This bodily, spiritual and mental unification is supposed to reveal to the human his or her origins, so that one can be enlightened and rediscover Godliness.

## FROM LONGING TO ENJOYMENT

How simple it would all be if there were a perfect aphrodisiac. It could be a little magic pill, that makes one irresistible, or a drop of a bewitching scent that confuses our senses. How alluring it would be to sprinkle a pinch of some powder into our partner's food - perhaps after years of being together - with the consequence that the partner suddenly becomes an expert in a wide variety of erotic delights. Boundless relaxation, shivers of lust through the whole body, orgasms that last much longer - it would be Utopia. Humans have been trying to find this place for centuries.

Modern love is dictated by speed. Few who are plagued by stress have time for prolonged sex. The pressure of modern life encourages minute-long 'quickies' and one-night-stands, lacking in fantasy. One expects aphrodisiacs to work with a correspondingly quick kick and visible success. Drugs, therefore, promise the best results: alcohol of course, marijuana and now Viagra. Those who are not afraid to risk banned substances will take cocaine, LSD and ecstasy.

Despite Spanish flies and impotence aids, ecstasy and medical preparations, the perfect aphrodisiac does not exist to date. There are, however, plants with narcotic effects, seasonings which stimulate, smokes that excite, and numerous drugs. The motto should be: 'the journey is the destination'. This book is a pointer to that which is closer: the desire for naked flesh, the sensual closeness of food and eroticism, the longing for it and the yearning for even more. It was mostly the belief in the efficacy of aphrodisiacs that achieved the required results and founded their reputations. Elixirs of love, eroticising and stimulating foods promise the rebirth of the slackened flesh and is aimed mainly at men.

'Hence I stumble from longing to enjoyment, and in the enjoyment I pine for longing' commented Johann Wolfgang von Goethe. He was not the first to relate his thoughts about the lust of flesh. To nibble or to feast, whether secretly or openly, to try strange or, even better, forbidden things, promises unusual titillations of the palate. Lust, at least in our fantasies, is the kingdom of wildest dreams and insatiable longing.

Only lust is never home-made. Temptation always seems to come in from outside. Pictures, music, and smells are forerunners of luck. Little tit-bits promise greater enjoyment than a paradisiacal and unexpected banquet. Exotic, enticing delicacies and tempting little obscenities? Clever or simple, piquant or classical? Italian, French or Japanese, Beluga caviar or potato pancakes with apple purée? The correct amount of time and the presentation are important, to suit every disposition.

A small, carefully composed gourmet menu with three courses, high in vitamins and minerals, fresh herbs and light sauces, is most suitable as an amorous appetiser. A romantic dinner can be a temptation par excellence, and a large banquet can work wonders.

Love, whether physical or emotional, is not, never was and never will be simple. The door to the Garden of Eden remains closed. In the desperate yearning, in the significance attributed to the search for the lost paradise of the senses, there lies a grain of that which is being sought. Sometimes, it seems that a wisp of air blows over to us through the cracks of the door of paradise.

# APHRODISIACS

## APHRODITE - GODDESS OF LOVE

It was no ordinary sea-foam which gave birth to Aphrodite, the Goddess of love and temptation, but rather it was the last act of Uranus' castrated penis. Greek mythology tells of the difficult union between the God of the Sky and Gaia, the original Goddess of Earth. Together, they had twelve children; six male and six female Titans. However, all their offspring were so deformed that Uranus stamped eleven of them back into the body of the earth. When their final son, Kronos, was born, Gaia swore to wreak revenge for the treatment of her children. She sent the child away to be given a safe upbringing, and when he came back, she gave her son a sickle, so that he could remove Uranus' manhood, should he approach her with sexual desires again. The time came, and the job was carried out. The mighty penis was thrown into the sea, and from the spot where it landed, the Goddess of Love was born.

'Aphro' means foam. The waves played with the severed phallus and, out of the foaming sperm, Aphrodite appeared, beautiful, perfect in stature and movement, and sensuous down to her last detail. A mussel shell carried the naked beauty to the shores of Cyprus in a floating procession accompanied by sparrows and pigeons. Roses blossomed on her arrival; wherever she trod, flowers and scented herbs sprouted. The island turned into a sea of flowers and even wild animals became gentle when they saw her.

Hesiod described Aphrodite as 'one who was the laugh of lovers (actually: the genitals of those who would like to love), because she was created from genitals'. The Goddess 'bore a longing for love in her breast and she went straight away to the shade of the valley to mate,' Homer sang. She even caused Zeus to lose his mind and managed to get him to 'willingly couple with mortal women'. Sexual excess, misunderstanding, confusion, erotic aberrations between animals, humans and gods - Aphrodite managed it all.

She owned a magic belt that was filled with every ingredient possible for the kindling of love and raising sexual desire, as well as the art of temptation and potency. In order to have access to these aphrodisiacs, the Greeks built a temple for Aphrodite and begged for her favour. As offerings, they brought her birds, above all sparrows and pigeons, prolific hares and the randy stag. They smothered her statue with scented flowers and herbs, pomegranates, quinces, roses, mint and myrrh. And they feasted in her name on strong, intoxicating drinks and tasty food.

## FROM THE WOMB OF NATURE TO THE KINGDOM OF THE SENSES

**Angels' trumpet:** angels' trumpet is a plant used by Native Americans in shamanic rituals and for healing. The plant has hallucinogenic properties due to the tropane alkaloids found in all parts of the plant.

***Where found:*** *South America and Europe.*

***Obtainable from:*** *specialist herb shops supply seeds, and the plant is found growing in many European gardens.*

***How to use:*** *as a drink (seeds, brewed in water or maize-beer)*

***Effect:*** *strong narcotic, hallucinations.*

**Aniseed:** this healing plant is a popular aphrodisiac and has many culinary uses, and has been used as far back as the Greeks and Romans. Its pleasant smelling oil not only improves food and drinks, but also makes them healthier. Popular belief allotted aniseed special powers: he who washed with aniseed retained his youthful appearance. 'Aniseed brings women milk and increases their desire to be immodest' (Leonhard Fuchs, New Herbal Book, 1543).

***Where found:*** *Europe, especially Eastern Mediterranean.*

***Obtainable from:*** *good delicatessens (fresh) and widely available in dried form.*

***How to use:*** *as a seasoning and healing aid (fresh or dried) for drinks and food.*

***Effect:*** *encourages digestion, stimulates nervous system and alleviates cramps.*

**Asparagus:** the Chinese use asparagus to alleviate coughs; the Egyptians value it as a food and the Greeks use it as a medicine for the kidneys. The pale, phallus-shaped spears are, above all, thought to have a stimulating, aphrodisiac effect. The most valuable part for medicinal use is the root.

***Where found:*** *worldwide.*

***Obtainable from:*** *Food Shops. Asparagus is traditionally a seasonal vegetable, available in early spring, but nowadays it is available throughout the year.*

***How to use:*** *as a vegetable. Asparagus is best steamed, or used in soup.*

***Effect:*** *diuretic.*

**Aubergine:** due to its shape, the aubergine (egg-plant) along with other members of the nightshade family to be an aphrodisiac. In Italy it is sometimes said that the aubergine can rob the eater of his sanity.

***Where found:*** *South-east Asia, Mediterranean.*

***Obtainable from:*** *widely available in supermarkets throughout the year*

***How to use:*** *as a vegetable*

***Effect:*** *enlivening and invigorating*

**Avocado:** Avocados probably originate from the Yucatan Peninsula in Mexico and there is evidence that the ancient Maya people cultivated the trees. Although no aphrodisiac effect has been demonstrated, both the stone (in the form of avocado oil) and the flesh are thought to be sexually stimulating. In addition, the avocado plays an important role in Native American traditional medicine, as a treatment for fevers, herpes and gynaecological problems.

***Where found:*** *Central America, tropical and sub-tropical regions, Southern Europe.*

***Obtainable from:*** *food shops around the year.*

***How to use:*** *as a fruit*

***Effect:*** *energy giving, revitalising*

**Basil:** there are a number of varieties of basil, and some are better suited to culinary uses, and others to medicinal use. Ocimum sanctum, a variety found in India is one of a group of plants considered to be holy to some Hindus, who according to their religion should eat one leaf a day. Ocimum basilicum (sweet basil) stimulates the sex-drive, and boosts fertility, and produces a general sense of well-being through the essential oils found in the leaves, tannins and vitamin content.

***Where found:*** *South Asia, Southern Europe.*

***Obtainable from:*** *food shops as a dried herb, although fresh basil is always preferable. It can be grown in a sunny garden, or found at most supermarkets.*

***How to use:*** *as a seasoning, brewed as a tea, smoked (in dried form).*

***Effect:*** *stimulating*

**Belladonna:** In the past, belladonna was considered to be a very powerful and magical plant. Wiccan witches would prepare highly effective love-potions and wines from the belladonna root.

Belladonna means beautiful woman, and the name of this plant results comes from the dilation of the pupils that occurs when the active substance (atropine) is ingested.

*Where found : Eurasia and North Africa.*

***Obtainable from:*** *wild plants growing in woodlands; seeds can be obtained from herbalists or head shops.*

***How to use:*** *belladonna can be eaten as a fruit, or the leaves can be smoked.* ***Important note:*** *the entire plant contains alkaloids, including atropine, which in the correct dosage can increase sexual excitement. However too much can lead to breathing difficulties, and even death - the fatal dose of atropine for humans is 0.1g, and it should be appreciated that it can be difficult to judge the correct number of berries to take, as atropine levels may vary between different berries*

***Effect:*** *strong aphrodisiac and hallucinations.*

**Betel nut:** In Asia, the seeds of the areca nut palm is widely enjoyed as food, and is also used medicinally. Betel nuts are most commonly eaten in a 'paan'. The nut is grated, and is put into a fresh betel leaf along with an assortment of other spices such as nutmeg, cloves and pepper with lime. This is then chewed for around 10 minutes, but not normally swallowed.

***Where found:*** *South East Asia and other tropical areas.*

***Obtainable from:*** *Asian shops as well as head shops stock the leaves, nuts and powder.*

***How to use:*** *Roll the nut up in a paan, use as a seasoning, or use the powder in a tea.*

*Effects: Reduces stress, anti-bacterial, stimulates, enlivens.*

**Calmus:** since olden times the roots of the calmus plant, which is similar to a reed, have been used in medicinal baths as well as being smoked. Traditionally, Native Americans would chew calmus to relieve fatigue, or they would powder it and take it as a snuff. Calmus contains a substance similar to mescaline, called isoasarone. In high doses, calmus is an aphrodisiac. The roots are collected in spring and late autumn and are then washed and dried. The roots should be stored in a cool and dry place, and they can be used for up to a year after being harvested.

***Where found:*** *originally in Southern Asia, today worldwide.*

***Obtainable from:*** *the banks of ponds and slow running rivers, where it grows wild; dried roots can be purchased from herbalists (Western or Chinese) or head shops.*

***How to use:*** *as a snack (roots, doses between 5-25 cm length of root), or added to tea or alcohol.*

***Effect:*** *stimulating, hallucinogenic. A bath with calmus powder added to the water can be an effective aphrodisiac.*

**Carrots:** The carrot has been associated with stimulation since ancient times, because of their vitamin content, and possibly because of their shape. In Asia carrots are eaten as a substitute for ginseng.

***Where found:*** *worldwide*

***Where obtainable****: widely available in food shops, and can be grown in the garden.*

***How to use:*** *as a vegetable (raw or cooked) or as a juice.*

***Effect:*** *raises energy levels, encourages sexual intercourse, diuretic.*

**Cardamom:** In ancient times cardamom was used as a herb, healing agent and aphrodisiac. Cardamom is related to ginger.

***Where found:*** *South East Asia.*

***Obtainable from:*** *most supermarkets in dried form, and fresh in Asian shops.*

***How to use:*** *as a spice on cooking, or added to coffee.*

***Effect:*** *stimulates and enlivens.*

**Celery:** valued as a foodstuff, celery is also known as an aphrodisiac in Europe. Celery roots are said to increase sexual stamina and celery root salad is supposed to work wonders on impotence.

***Where found:*** *worldwide.*

***Obtainable from:*** *food shops.*

***How to use:*** *as a vegetable, seasoning (as celery seeds).*

***Effect:*** *stimulant.*

**Chilli:** chilli is a variety of paprika, and is used as a vegetable and seasoning as an integral part of Indian cuisine. Chilli is considered to be a 'hot' food, not just because of its taste, but also because it stimulates sexual urges. Capsaicin, the substance that makes chilli hot, irritates and stimulates the mucous membranes.

***Where found:*** *Central and South America*

***Obtainable from:*** *supermarkets and delicatessens.*

***How to use:*** *as seasoning (fresh, dried) - be careful not to use too much.*

***Effect:*** *stimulating*

**Cinnamon:** 2,800 years ago, cinnamon was first mentioned in the Chinese emperor's herbal book. The dried rind of the cinnamon tree is used to season sweet dishes and mulled wine. Thick, spicy-smelling cinnamon oil is distilled from the rind and leaves, and is used to guard against colds. Cinnamon oil rubbed onto the genitals produces a very strong aphrodisiacal effect.

***Where found:*** *South-east Asia.*

***Obtainable from:*** *supermarkets.*

***How to use:*** *as a seasoning in food and drinks, the oil can be added to a hot bath and can also be rubbed into the skin.*

***Effect:*** *powerful anti-bacterial agent, encourages the appetite, regulates the menstrual cycle.*

**Cloves:** The dried green buds of the clove have been considered to be an aphrodisiac for well over five thousand years. The Chinese used to chew cloves during erotic escapades, to ensure pleasant breath. Clove oil contains eugenol, which has a mildly psychedelic effect. Cloves also have narcotic and antiseptic qualities; it is still used as a medicine against mild toothache.

***Where found:*** *cultivated in tropical zones.*

***Obtainable from:*** *food shops.*

***How to use:*** *as a seasoning or oil.*

***Effect:*** *stimulating.*

**Coca:** The leaves of the coca bush were widely used in Peru, long before Incan times. Cocaine is derived from the leaves, and is used in the West as a sensory stimulant and euphoric. Used on a localised part of the body, cocaine or coca leaf paste has a numbing effect. Anal intercourse was not considered to be 'unnatural' in Peru, but was practised by both homosexual and heterosexual partners; coca paste was rubbed onto the anus beforehand. Coca was used medicinally as an analgesic, against mountain sickness and as an appetite suppressant. It is still widely used today, and many South Americans prepare the leaves with ash and dissolved lime and chew the leaves.

In 1863, the Corsican chemist, Angelo Mariani, patented a drink made from wine and coca leaves. 23 years later the pharmacist, John S. Pemberton from Georgia developed a refreshing, stimulating drink, which was to become the symbol of the western world: Coca-Cola. However, the extract of the cola nut and coca leaves have long been removed from the ingredient list and have been replaced by a higher doses of caffeine.

Sigmund Freud's publication about his experiments with coca in 1884 led to the snorting of cocaine becoming quite fashionable in artistic circles in Europe. However, cocaine is addictive, and not all users would share Gottfried Benn's enthusiasm for how cocaine causes the 'sweet disintegration of the individual'. Many users suffer from depression following the 'come down'. Cocaine no longer enjoys a romantic image, but it is widely used illegally throughout the West.

***Where found:*** *South America.*

***Obtainable from:*** *cocaine is illegal, and cannot be legally possessed, bought or sold.*

***How to use:*** *cocaine powder is snorted, and the coca leaves can be chewed.*

***Effect:*** *very strong stimulant.*

**Cocoa:** It was the 'nourishment of the Gods' according to the Indians and a much-loved aphrodisiac. The Aztecs grated the roasted beans, mixed them with maize flour, chilli, vanilla, pimento, pepper, rolls of cinnamon bark and pumpkin seeds, and added cold or warm water. Either salted or sweetened with honey, they formed a chocolate. Europeans also valued chocolate: 'One obtained strength from chocolate for certain tasks' said a text from the 17th century. Cocoa contains a related substance to caffeine, namely theobromine.

***Where found:*** *Central America, Asia, Africa.*

*Where obtainable: food shops.*

***How to use:*** *as a drink (grated beans)*

***Effect:*** *slightly stimulating.*

**Coconut Palm:** the coconut palm is a very useful plant - not only is the fruit (coconut) edible, but medicine is obtained from the roots and the flower stems can be tapped to extract palm wine. One palm can produce 400 litres of juice in a week, and this is widely considered to be an aphrodisiac in many parts of the world. Its effect is enhanced by adding apple seeds and honey. The coconut flesh is also supposed to have a stimulating effect.

***Where found:*** *throughout the tropics.*

***Obtainable from:*** *food shops for coconuts, milk and palm wine in Asian shops.*
*How to eat: as fruit and as palm wine.*
***Effect:*** *strengthens, intoxicating.*

**Coffee**: the brew made from roasted coffee beans was once a holy drink; due to its stimulating effects, it was used by African Sufis during meditation.
***Where found:*** *East Africa, Arabia.*
***Obtainable from:*** *food shops.*
***How to use:*** *brew freshly ground coffee as a drink; do not use instant powder. If being used as an aphrodisiac, coffee can be spiced up with honey and cardamom.*
***Effect:*** *powerfully enlivening.*

**Coriander:** this herb was well-known in olden days in Egypt and Palestine as an effective aphrodisiac. As a seasoning in wine, coriander was thought to increase sperm production.
***Where found:*** *worldwide.*
***Obtainable from:*** *most food shops as a powder, seeds and fresh in Asian shops.*
***How to use:*** *as a seasoning (seeds and leaves).*
***Effect:*** *enlivening.*

**Cress:** All edible types of cress - water cress, garden cress and Indian cress - have a high vitamin C content and help to maintain general well-being. Indian cress is reputedly good as an aphrodisiac purely due to the distinct colouring of its leaves.
***Where found:*** *worldwide.*
***Obtainable from:*** *food shops.*
***How to use:*** *as a salad.*
***Effect:*** *energizing.*

**Date palm:** Five thousand years ago, in Mesopotamia the date palm was cultivated and used as food and a drug. Juice was tapped from the stem, which upon beingn left, would become an intoxicating drink. Probably mixed with other drugs, this drink was served at temple dances and at erotic rituals.

***Where found:*** *Asia Minor, Arabia, North Africa*

***Obtainable from:*** *food shops as a fruit, as date wine in Asian shops.*

***How to use:*** *as a fruit, as date wine.*

***Effect:*** *energy giving, intoxicating.*

**Figs:** the fig has been considered for centuries to be a symbol of fertility, due its shape and amount of seeds. It is no coincidence that the fig leaf has been used to cover the genitals of those embarrassed by their nakedness.

***Where found:*** *Mediterranean area, sub-tropical and tropical regions.*

***Obtainable from:*** *food shops.*

***How to use:*** *as a fruit (fresh or dried), or as juice.*

***Effect:*** *refreshing.*

**Fennel:** fennel originates from the Mediterranean area and was grown by the Greeks and Romans for medicinal and culinary purposes. In the Middle Ages, fennel was said to possess magical aphrodisiac qualities. In medicine it was used for improving eyesight and to guard against indigestion.

***Obtainable from:*** *own garden, bulbs in food shops, seeds in specialist herb shops.*

***How to use:*** *as seasoning (seeds), as greens (leaves) as vegetable (bulb).*

***Effect:*** *refreshing*

**Garlic:** garlic was thought of in ancient Egypt as a healing aid that worked wonders and at the same time acted as a stimulant. The Romans dedicated it to Ceres, the Goddess of fertility. Mixed with coriander, garlic juice was served as a love potion to cure impotence caused by witchcraft and to encourage illicit liaisons. However, the unpleasant breath that results from eating garlic is enough to make close contact repellent for some people.

'He who during the battle of love cannot prove himself to be a man eats garlic and is then really strong. If an elderly woman is tired, then she does not hesitate to eat garlic as well, and the gentle Venus will laugh about your battle in a friendly way.' Roman quotation

***Where found:*** *worldwide.*
***Obtainable from:*** *food shops.*
***How to use:*** *as a herb (raw, cooked or crushed), tincture or tablet.*
***Effect:*** *makes one feel younger, strengthens, antibiotic properties, activates cells.*

**Ginger:** ginger is a tropical and subtropical cultivated plant, resembling reeds (which are also sold as a healing agent). The roots contain an essential oil, which give it its characteristic flavour as a spicy herb. In Arabian countries, coffee is often spiced up using ginger.

***Where found:*** *Southern Asia.*
***Obtainable from:*** *food shops.*
***How to use:*** *as a herb (fresh or dried, as powder, pressed, grated or preserved in syrup), as a refreshing drink (ginger-ale), beer or liqueur.*
***Effect:*** *enlivens, encourages digestion, stimulates.*

**Ginseng:** the ginseng root (Chinese: human root) is considered the oldest and most sought after aphrodisiac and healing agent in Asia. As far back as 2500 BC, the doctor Shen-Nung used its enormous powers. In medicine, it has lost none of its value even today. In Chinese healing, harmonising medicines are preferred. Influenced by the Taoist school, it is thought that both the cosmic powers - Yin (female) and Yang (male) - become equal, in order to prevent sickness and malfunctioning of the human body. As a general healing aid this 'root of the heavens' is supposed to assist in acquiring eternal life. However, it is not suitable for the quick kick: the effect of ginseng unfolds only when taken regularly over a long period of time. For spontaneous reactions there are other options: ginseng, taken with musk, opium (illegal of course), prawn powder, and ginger. He who makes pills from these and half an hour before coitus chews one, 'will experience a true wonder'.

It's root form is highly efficacious. It is said that the more they resemble the penis, the more explosive the effect, although ginseng is not commonly found in this form. Experienced ginseng hunters also know the rituals and legends connected with this plant: A spirit, in human form, is supposed to live in every root and it unites erotically with the collector. Only the collector knows how he must handle the plant demons, whether to praise them or be cunning, by chanting prayers or magic sayings. The Chinese character for ginseng is the same as for potency.

***Where found:*** *East Asia.*

***Obtainable from:*** *from Asian shops in fresh form, as tablets, tincture or extract in chemists or drug-stores.*

***How to use:*** *fresh, either chewed or as tea. Some people place ginseng extract in alcohol for at least three months before using.*

***Effect:*** *universal healing agent, strengthens and stimulates if taken regularly.*

**Guarana:** the seeds of this liana vine are also called 'fruits of youth'. It makes a refreshing drink, which is a powerful stimulant. The seeds contain caffeine, resin and essential oil.

***Where found:*** *the Amazonian basin.*
***Obtainable from:*** *health food shops, head shops.*
***How to use:*** *as a drink (boil the seeds), tincture, chewing gum, chocolate, paste.*

**Hemp:** hemp is one of the oldest plants known to humanity, and is used as a source of fibre and oil. It is also used to produce hashish and marijuana. The psychoactive effect associated with marijuana is caused by the THC (tetrahydrocannibinol) content of the plant, along with other cannabinoids. Among many users, cannabis has the reputation of being one of the best aphrodisiacs in the world.

The 'grass of ecstasy' is described in Indian's religious scripts as a holy plant, which not only helps to alleviate physical complaints, but also refreshes the mind and soul. As long ago as five thousand years, doctors used hemp against various ailments: lack of appetite, headaches, digestion problems and impotence. Its erotic importance is described in the legend about the godly pair, Shiva and Parvati. Shiva, much to the dismay of his wife, played around with other goddesses. During the search for something to bind her husband to her, she discovered the female hemp flower with its resin. She gave it to Shiva to smoke, who was filled with a new lust for his wife. Their heavenly ecstasy was so powerful, that from then on, Shiva resisted all other temptations.

'The spirit of hemp is the spirit of peace and knowledge. During hemp induced ecstasy, the lightening of eternity transforms the darkness of martyrdom into pure light.' Hemp is the 'giver of pleasure', 'the seventh heaven', 'heaven's leader', the 'heaven for the poor man', the 'comforter of mourning'. 'No God, no person is as good as the religious hemp drinker', were some of the verdicts of the British Hemp Drug Commission Report, in 1884.

Cannabis is used in drinks for Tantric love rituals. As with opium, the effect varies according to whether one smokes, eats or drinks the plant. For the wide variety of recipes there are several cannabis drugs at ones disposal: the dried female flower ('marijuana'), the resin from the flowers ('hashish'), fresh or dried leaves ('grass'). Ayurveda (meaning, knowledge of life) is an ancient Indian school of medicine, which recommended blends of hemp buds and other healing ingredients. One such recipe calls for hemp buds and leaves, hashish, opium and thorn apple. This mixture would be then added to various spices including cloves, cardamom, incense aniseed, caraway seeds, butter fat, flour, milk and sugar.

***Where found:*** *worldwide.*

***Note:*** *as a narcotic, hemp is an illegal drug.*

***How to use:*** *as an addition to food or as tea (resin), smoked (female flowers).*

***Effect:*** *mildly psychedelic, intensifies awareness, stimulates, increases appetite and sexual desire.*

**Henbane:** this poisonous night-shade plant, has been known since ancient times as a healing plant and was used in magic. Witches brewed amorous love potions from this highly effective plant containing tropane alkaloids. Henbane seeds and leaves would be smoked as an alleged cure for toothache, and in the Middle Ages, it was smoked as a stimulant by those visiting 'bathing houses'. Henbane could also be ground up and added to beer.

***Where found:*** *Eurasia, North Africa.*

***Obtainable from:*** *specialist herb shops, head shops, and can be found growing in the wild.*

***How to use:*** *smoke (leaves and seeds).*

*Note: eating the seeds are not recommended, as the alkaloids contained in the seeds can be fatal in high doses. Because henbane is a natural substance, the amount of alkaloids found in the seeds*

*can vary from plant to plant.*
***Effect:*** *reduces sexual inhibition, hallucinations and vivid dreams.*

**Honey:** Honey is crucial to most aphrodisiac drinks. The Maya Indians would add honey to nightshade or to various barks or even to the extracts of toads which have psychoactive properties. In Mexico, the honey of the stingless bee was a popular aphrodisiac, and in England, mead (honey wine) with extra honey added was regularly taken to increase the libido. Many products are derived from honey, including royal jelly, and propolis, which are considered to have many healing properties, including guarding against sterility and impotence.
***Where found:*** *worldwide.*
***Obtainable from:*** *food shops.*
***How to use:*** *on bread, or as mead.*
***Effect:*** *stimulates and strengthens.*

**Horseradish:** horseradish has been grown since the 12th century and is mainly used as a herb. Due to its resemblance to a penis, the root, and its use as a spicy seasoning, horseradish was credited with magic powers to prevent sexual exhaustion in men.
***Where found:*** *Europe.*
***Obtainable from:*** *food shops, and can be grown in one's own garden.*
***How to use:*** *as a seasoning.*
***Effect:*** *enlivens and strengthens. Also stimulates digestion.*

**Liquorice:** Liquorice contains, among other things, glycyrrhizin, essential oils and hormones which are used as an old folk remedy to cure coughs, stomach and bowel problems. It is said to be an aphrodisiac which stimulates women in particular.
***Where found:*** *South East Europe and South West Asia.*

***Obtainable from:*** *Asian shops and supermarkets.*
***How to use:*** *as a powder or tea.*
***Effect:*** *general tonic*

**Lovage:** The aphrodisiac effects of the leaves and roots of lovage have been known since ancient times. Love potions can be prepared from lovage roots.
***Where found:*** *Eurasia.*
***Obtainable from:*** *specialist herbal shops and can be grown in one's own garden.*
***How to use:*** *as seasoning or fresh as salad.*
***Effect:*** *enlivening and calmative.*

**Mandrake:** The effects of mandrake were discovered by the naturalist Paracelsus. It is a highly sought after and rare plant.

The roots are supposed to have magic powers; they were often used in magic and heathen rituals. Where the root was found, and what condition it was in would determine what magic use the root would be put to. In the Middle Ages, it was considered to be dangerous to harvest the roots; it was believed that if a layman pulled the roots out of the ground, the roots would emit a blood-curdling scream, which would kill the collector on the spot. To counteract this 'danger', a 'black, hungry dog' would be tied to the root with a string. In the dog's attempt to free itself, it would pull the root out, and if there was any danger, the dog would die rather than the harvester.

Whether as a drink, cream or talisman, its narcotic effect made the mandrake very popular. Many legends surround the root, which is also called Mandragora (Persian for love herb). 'This magical mandrake/ was grown by God and his saviour's forgotten people/ under the gallows and strung-up victims/it is said that after death of the hanged/ the urine and seeds grew/ in the form of a little penis.' (Acorn, 'The Knowledge of Magic',

1674). Mandrake has an anthropomorphic form. With a bit of imagination, one can make out both female and male sex organs. The Church, not surprisingly, viewed the plant as a threat and so damned and banned the plant; they saw potential for a pact with the Devil in the yearning for mandrake and the desire associated with it. In Joan of Arc's trial, reference was made to a talisman made from mandrake, which was worn by the brave French woman. Superstitions surrounding mandrake demanded scrupulous personal care: in order to keep the volatile spirit of the mandrake in good humour, it was thought that one should change one's clothes regularly and wash the roots in wine.

Originally, mandrake grew in the Near East, and the first recipes came from Papyrus. Next to deadly nightshade, henbane and the thorn apple, it was mixed into various love potions, including some enjoyed by Cleopatra. He who could not find the magical plant in Northern Europe, made do with allemann's root (Latin: allumm victorialis), yellow gentian or virginia creeper. The roots of all these plants contain highly powerful tropane alkaloids. Possible unpleasant side-effects when eating this plant are nausea and a dry mouth.

***Where found:*** *Southern Europe, North Africa, Himalayan regions, Asia Minor.*

***Obtainable from:*** *specialist herbalists, head shops and occasionally from garden centres.*

***How to use:*** *as a wine and tea (quarter to half a teaspoon of the root is considered to be a safe dose) The leaves can also be smoked.*

*Caution: in rare cases, overdoses can be fatal as a result of respiratory paralysis.*

***Effect:*** *lowers sexual inhibitions, stimulates and is mildly hallucinogenic.*

**Morels:** these mushrooms have been appreciated as aphrodisiacs for centuries in all cultural circles. This could be due to the resemblance they bear to a penis, but is more likely to do with their musky, smoky flavour. One can recognise a morel by its cap, which is full of little holes and resembles a sponge.
***Where found:*** *grows throughout the world during the spring in mountainous regions.*
***Obtainable from:*** *food shops and delicatessens either fresh, dried or preserved.*
*How to use. as a vegetable.*
***Effect:*** *enlivens and sensitises.*

**Mountain rush:** this plant was used in the Netherlands in ancient times as a central part in rituals. In China, the ephedrine plant (Ma-Huang) was an important natural medicine. Nearly every culture is aware of the aphrodisiac effects of tea made from the leaves of the plant.
***Where found:*** *worldwide.*
***Obtainable from:*** *chemists, specialist herb shops.*
***How to use:*** *as greens, tea (15-30g per litre water, boil for 10 min.)*
***Effect:*** *enlivens, helps breathing, anti-allergic, stimulates.*

**Muira Puama (Latin - Ptychopetaium olacoides):** South American Indians have known about this bushy tree for centuries, and it has been used as an aphrodisiac since its discovery. The bark and hard wood is boiled for hours to produce a love potion.
***Where found:*** *the Amazon basin.*
***Obtainable from:*** *head shops in the form of an alcohol extract.*
***How to use:*** *as a drink.*
***Effect:*** *extreme excitement, strengthens the nerves, increases potency*

**Muscatel sage:** this sage has been known since ancient times as a herb and healing aid. Mixed with wine, it increases sexual enjoyment. In aromatherapy, essential oil of sage, whose flavour is similar to amber, acts as an aphrodisiac if inhaled several times a day or if a few drops are taken internally.

***Where found:*** *Mediterranean regions*

***Obtainable from:*** *specialist herb shops.*

***How to use:*** *as a herb or as an essential oil. The dried leaves can be used pure or mixed with henbane, hemp or thorn apple and then smoked.*

***Effect:*** *sexually stimulating.*

**Mustard:** since olden times, mustard has been touted as being able to increase one's potency. The Roman Plinius, was convinced that if three leaves of the white mustard were picked with the left hand, then drunk in honey-water, it would increase sexual desire. It was forbidden for monks to eat mustard, as it was feared that the plant would lead them into temptation. There are three types of mustard: black, the Indian and white mustard. Black mustard has the most intense aroma.

***Where found:*** *Eurasia and North Africa.*

***Obtainable from:*** *food shops, and can be grown in one's own garden.*

***How to use:*** *as a seasoning (seeds or paste).*

***Effect:*** *stimulating, irritant.*

**Nettles:** For centuries, the nettle was known for their healing and nutritious properties even though the hairs on the leaves contain an irritating poison. In olden days, partners would whip each other with nettle plants to stimulate each other. The Roman poet Petronius maintained that men would retain their masculinity if they rubbed nettles on their navel, loins, and buttocks.

***Where found:*** *worldwide.*

***Obtainable from:*** *one's own garden or growing wild, herbalists and chemists.*

***How to use:*** *drink the leaves as a tea or dry them and smoke them in a rolled cigarette. The fresh leaves can be used as a substitute for spinach in casseroles (young, fresh leaves and stalks).*

***Effect:*** *stimulates the circulation, skin irritant (fresh leaves).*

**Nutmeg:** nutmeg is not really a nut but is actually a seed. Because of the stimulating sensory effects of this spice, it has been considered one of the most popular seasonings since the 16th century. Nutmeg has a psychoactive effect, which lasts up to twelve hours (taking effect between one and five hours after consumption), due to the high level of myristicin in the essential oils found in the seed. A bath with a few drops of nutmeg essential oil has a particularly stimulating effect. Myristicin forms the main basis for the fashionable synthesised drug of the nineties; MDMA (Ecstasy).

***Where found:*** *Asia, Africa, cultivated in all tropical zones.*

***Obtainable from:*** *food shops as a nut or fresh from Asian shops. The essential oil can be found in health food shops.*

***How to use:*** *as a spice, or as an essential oil in massage oil or in a bath. Dried, powdered nutmeg can also be smoked in a joint along with hemp.*

**Onions:** the onion is one of the oldest cultivated vegetables and as was one of the staple foods of the ancient Egyptians, who treated it as a holy plant. When the Israelis fled from Egypt, they missed the more than anything else from their diet. For the Greeks and Romans the onion was a medicinal vegetable, as a cure for coughs and colds. Onions were as highly esteemed as garlic, as both were believed to be an aphrodisiac and symbol of fertility.

***Where found:*** *worldwide*

***Obtainable from:*** *food shops.*
***How to use:*** *as a vegetable or as a herb (in powdered form).*
***Effect:*** *highly antibacterial, stimulating.*

**Orchis:** Paraclesus first discovered the effect of orchis as an aphrodisiac. This member of the orchid family is a well-known aphrodisiac in Europe and the Orient. Paracelsus maintained that after eating orchis just once, a man 'could have an erection' twelve times. It was probably supposed that they had an effect on the male genitals because their knobbly roots resembled testicles. This is backed up by the mention of the orchis root in Greek mythology: Orchis (Greek for testicles), was the son of a nymph and a satyr. When he was killed, he was born again, in the form of a beautiful orchid. Satyrs would eat orchis, and the mythical creatures, which were half ram and half human would become so lusty that they would apparently spray sperm onto the floor!

Orchis was harvested for magical rituals and served with drinks and food. The Indians also considered the bulbs useful for increasing sperm production.

***Where found:*** *Europe and the Orient.*
***Obtainable from:*** *specialist garden centres.*
***Note:*** *in many countries, orchis is a protected species.*
***How to use:*** *the powdered roots can be used as a flour.*
***Effect:*** *strengthening*

**Parsley:** Since olden days, parsley has been widely used as a herb, the root being a medicinal aid. In ancient times, it was considered that the plant was a symbol of reincarnation; rumour had it that the plant was capable of creating new life. In the Middle Ages the stalk was used to make lover's magic; the roots were mixed with an enticing cream, and applied to produce ecstasy. The roots and seeds contain an essential oil, with the main ingredient being apiol.

***Where found:*** *cultivated worldwide*
***Obtainable from:*** *food shops, and can be grown in one's own garden.*
***How to use:*** *as seasoning or as a drink, (oil and root extract).*
***Note:*** *if pregnant, high doses can cause abortion.*
***Effect:*** *stimulating, slightly enlivening, diuretic. Parsley enhances one's moods, and in high doses is a strong sexual stimulant.*

**Pepper:** For the Indians, pepper is the 'king of herbs'. It was used thousands of years before our time and later brought to Europe by Alexander the Great. Pepper has influenced cultural history and, in its name, battles have been fought and human lives lost. This, the most famous of all herbs is considered in Asia and Europe to be an aphrodisiac, encouraging sexual intercourse, although higher doses can irritate the mucous membranes.

For a long time Arabia ruled the herbal market and brought new recipes for 'kindling sexual lust' to the West. Some herbs were as expensive as gold. False samples - in particular of pepper, saffron and nutmeg - got so out of hand and were considered so socially dangerous that, in the Holy Roman Empire, cheating in spice dealing was punishable by death until 1440.

The standard mixture, that can be sprinkled over just about any meal, and 'does not allow the fire of love ever to go out', was recommended by the doctor Moses Maimonides (1135-1204). His recipe was 1 ounce of long pepper, 1 ounce of galangal root, 2 ounces of cinnamon, 2 ounces of aniseed, 1/2 ounce of mace and 1/2 ounce of nutmeg. (1 oz = 25g)

***Where found:*** *Southern Asia.*
***Obtainable from:*** *food shops, and special herbal mixtures from specialist herbalists and head shops.*
***How to use:*** *as a herb or spice.*
***Effect:*** *stimulates, encourages circulation.*

**Pimento:** Traditional Native American medicine uses the fruit and leaves of the pimento tree to treat neuralgia, digestive problems and for warming the body. It kindles lust and is a popular addition to cocoa.

***Where found:*** *Central America, Caribbean.*
***Obtainable from:*** *delicatessens and food shops.*
***How to use:*** *as a herb.*
***Effect:*** *stimulating.*

**Pineapple:** This tropical fruit contains an enzyme called Bromelin, which encourages the digestion of protein. Additionally, pinapples are rich in vitamin C and minerals. It is considered to be an aphrodisiac when eaten with the unlikely accompaniment of chilli powder or when soaked in rum with honey; a small measure a day is said to increase potency.

***Where found:*** *South America.*
***Obtainable from:*** *food stores.*
***How to use:*** *as fresh fruit or as juice.*
***Note:*** *unripe fruit can cause miscarriage.*
***Effect:*** *Strengthening, diuretic, rids one of poisons.*

**Pomegranates:** Throughout Europe and Asia, the pomegranate is a symbol of vitality and immortality. It was valued as a lover's gift. Adam and Eve ate from the tree of knowledge, and became aware of their nakedness and the difference between good and evil, which led to the door of paradise being slammed in their faces. The tree is commonly described as being an apple tree, but because of the supposed location of Eden, it is more likely that the tree of knowledge was a pomegranate tree. The fruit was considered in olden days to be an 'apple of love' and was dedicated to Aphrodite as well as Zeus's wife, Hera. The tree stood as a symbol of Godly unification with man and the consumption of the fruit and seeds were correspondingly effective. The brilliantly red fruit with its many seeds symbolise, like figs, the womb and fertility.

In his book of herbs of 1562, the Italian doctor and man of letters, Matthiolus, recommended: 'For a medicine of some delicacy against the bad ailments and orifices of the secret places of men and women, take the rind of a pomegranate and a sponge, dry out both and grind to powder, and sprinkle on the problem.'

***Where found:*** *Asia minor.*

***Obtainable from:*** *supermarkets and delicatessens.*

***How to use:*** *as a fruit or juice (grenadine).*

***Effect:*** *energy giving.*

**Poppy seeds:** The poppy is a plant that has been cultivated since the dawning of human history. Opium was extracted from the sap of the seeds pods of the opium poppy, and was considered to be a plant blessed by the gods (the Greek word opus meaning juice). From the poppy, some of the oldest medicines, analgesics and aphrodisiacs have been produced. The poppy contains a complex mixture of alkaloids, the most well known being morphine. Other poppy-derived alkaloids such as codeine, thebaine, papaverine and narcotine play an important role in the narcotic effects of opium.

The healing powers of the sap were known as long ago as 4,500 years ago. Where this plant originated from is unclear but one of the ancient centres for growing and producing opium was Cyprus and the Island of Aphrodite. According to Theocrat, the intoxicating opium juice came from the tears of the Goddess of Love, as she cried for the loss of her loved one, Adonis. Other Greek Gods were also associated with the poppy seed: Hypnos, the God of Sleep; his son Morpheus, the provider of dreams, and Dionysos, the God of Intoxication. Nyx, the Goddess of the Night and Ruler of Space was given a string of powers.

Just before the pod fully ripens, it is slit. This always takes place in the evening, so that the milky residue can seep out and dry over night, to be collected the following morning.

Though illegal, opium is either smoked or eaten. Different cultures use different additives in order to get optimal results and to reduce the side-effects including several nightshade plants, herbs, wine and other types of alcohol. As a stimulant, opium is only effective in small doses, as Krunitz wrote in 1805: 'Another result of blood mobilised by opium is an awakened and increased lust for sexual intercourse that is so great that even old men feel the effect; and the penises of slaughtered Turks in battle were still erect: also the nightly escape of sperm was common with the lusty thoughts. However, a too great a loss made men incapable of intercourse.'

The Arabs were probably the first to discover the powers of the 'pleasure plant'. They brought it to Greece, India and China. In order that opium could produce colourful, erotic dreams, it was mixed with special fermented opium (Chinese Tschandu) before being smoked. Pressed into the shape of little fish the mixture was sold in the markets. The fish symbolises fertility and life in Chinese tradition, but it also represented, as in Italy, the penis. The saying 'fish and water come together' refers to sexual intercourse. Some historians maintain that the fertility of the Chinese people is a result of its consumption of opium.

***Where found:*** *worldwide.*

***Obtainable from:*** *some shops will sell opium poppy seeds. Normal red poppy seeds are widely available, although their effect is much weaker.*

***Note:*** *growing opium poppy seeds is illegal. Taking opium and its derivatives is illegal without a prescription.*

***How to use:*** *smoke, chew or snort (powder)*

***Effect:*** *intoxicating, sexually stimulating.*

**Pumpkin:** pumpkin seeds are highly valued in India as an aphrodisiac, and they play a significant role in certain Tantric love rituals. It is said that if a woman eats pumpkin or melon seeds, she is showing her willingness for sex. The flowers and flesh of the pumpkin are thought to have aphrodisiac qualities.

***Where found:*** *worldwide.*
***Obtainable from:*** *food shops.*
***How to use:*** *As fruit, or snack (seeds).*

**Rosemary:** rosemary has been used dried as incense as well as a seasoning for wine. This evergreen plant was considered to be a plant of death as well as of love, which further highlights the association between orgasm and death. Traditionally, brides wore a wreath made from rosemary. Shakespeare's Ophelia also knew about its deep symbolic value: 'And there is rosemary, which stands for faithfulness'. The rosemary which is found in northern Eurasia (Ledum palustre), was used by shamans as a magical herb.

***Where found:*** *Eurasia, North Africa, cultivated world-wide.*
***Obtainable from:*** *food shops and can be grown in one's own garden.*
***How to use:*** *as a herb.*
*Note: in high doses rosemary can cause miscarriage.*
***Effect:*** *stimulates circulation, encourages digestion. A bath with rosemary essential oil stimulates, and encourages blood to flow through the skin so increasing sensitivity.*

**Saffron:** the Greeks believed that saffron aroused female lust. In the Islamic medicine, the male pistils of the crocus flower are dried, and the spice is considered to have 'heating' qualities, supposedly increasing the sexual desire of young men and strengthening the female uterus. The essential oils which contain activating and stimulating properties, it also became a substitute for opium. Weight-for- weight it is more valuable than gold.

***Where found:*** *Asia Minor and North Africa.*

***Obtainable from:*** *food shops.*

***How to use:*** *as a herb.*

***Note:*** *high doses of saffron can result in toxic poisoning and can cause miscarriages.*

***Effect:*** *stimulating and intoxicating. Intense and long orgasms can result.*

**Sunflowers:** sunflowers have been cultivated in gardens in Europe since the 16th century, for their beauty as well as their healing powers and nutritional properties. The leaves as well as the flower petals are considered a healing agent for rheumatism and stomach and bowel ailments. The Mayas boiled the flower petals and drank the tea because of its stimulating effect, caused by the presence of chlorogen-acids.

***Where found:*** *worldwide.*

***Obtainable from:*** *one's own garden, or as seeds from health shops.*

***How to use:*** *as a flour, as a snack (seeds), as tea (petals), as oil.*

***Effect:*** *stimulating.*

**Tea :** as with coffee or cocoa, tea is commonly drunk for enjoyment throughout the world. Taoists drank it as a popular stimulant as well as for meditative purposes. Combined with other ingredients such as herbs, wine, ginseng or opium, tea was also considered an aphrodisiac. Paradoxically, the shorter the brewing time, the more stimulating the effect is.

***Where found:*** *Asia.*

*Where obtainable: tea and food-shops, fresh from Asian shops.*

***How to use:*** *brew in hot water*

***Effect:*** *stimulating.*

**Truffles:** these mushrooms are the rarest and most sensual of fungi. Collete, the French author wrote: 'Its magnificent taste will solve all difficulties and problems'.

***Where found:*** *truffles grows underground in the shade of oak trees in the Dordogne, Alsace, Provence, Italy and North Africa.*
***Obtainable from:*** *delicatessens, fresh or preserved.*
***How to use:*** *as a vegetable.*
***Effect:*** *stimulating and sensitising.*

**Vanilla:** *The scent and flavour of vanilla is said to increase lust, especially when combined with cocoa or arrowroot. The etymology of the word 'vanilla' comes from the same stem as 'vagina' and homeopathic doctors prescribe vanilla as a cure for impotence all over the world.*

***Where found:*** *Central America.*
***Obtainable from:*** *food shops.*
***How to use:*** *as a tincture or herb.*
***Effect:*** *stimulating and energy giving.*

**Vermouth:** this is one of the oldest healing plants for gynaecological complaints and in olden days the Vermouth plant was dedicated to the young Goddess Artemis. Its branches were used in love potions and the dried leaves were smoked as a substitute for marijuana. Absinthe, brandy made from vermouth, flavoured with aniseed and fennel, became the notorious drug of the bohemians in the 19th century. The leaves of the plant contains the psychedelic, stimulating substance called thujon, which can also be toxic.

***Where found:*** *Eurasia, North Africa, America.*
***Obtainable from:*** *one's own garden, dried in specialist herbal shops and in chemists.*
***How to use:*** *as absinthe or smoked (leaves)*
***Effect:*** *slightly psychedelic.*

**Wine:** along with other forms of alcohol, wine is without doubt the world's most important and widely-used drug. It is often used for ritual purposes, to experience ecstasy. Wine has been said to be a wonderful aphrodisiac and holy drink since olden times. Cleopatra used it, mixed with raw opium and various nightshade plants, to achieve total lack of inhibitions.

Grapes were cultivated over five thousand years ago in Mesopotamia. The cult surrounding the intoxicating liquid reached its peak in Greece. To honour the God Dionysus, mass orgies were held, where wine flowed in rivers. However, the holy wine was not drunk pure by the Dionysus' followers: Vermouth, hyssop, thyme, laurel, myrrh, crocus and marjoram oil, mint, juniper, pepper, henbane, thorn apple, hellebore and opium raised the level of intoxication. It was so strong, that the wine had to be well diluted with water, otherwise revellers would have gone mad and remained so.

***Where found:*** *worldwide*

***Obtainable from:*** *off-licences, food shops and wine shops.*

***How to use:*** *as wine.*

***Effect:*** *intoxicating, relaxing.*

# RECIPES

*All recipes, unless otherwise stated, are for two people.*

## FOREPLAY

*They are dining in their favourite restaurant. A French restaurant, with white tablecloths, folded linen napkins, much silver, precious crystal, chandeliers and flowers everywhere. Extravagance in high ceilinged rooms; pure luxury. Just then, the thief interrupted his verbose soliloquy with a relishing and satisfying burp. Georgina filled the pause with a soft voice: "Gourmets don't burp."*

*A man sits at the neighbouring table, completely immersed in a book. Eats as if by the way, and does not register the food falling from his fork - Georgina watches him in an amused way. She sees him guiding the empty fork to his open lips. Only when the metal touches his mouth does he look up and he meets her quiet smile. They look at each other, judging, curiously touching each other with glances.*

*The thief speaks: "Money is my business, and eating my pleasure. Georgina is also my pleasure. Of course on a much more private level". Laughs loudly and gropes for her under the table. "One must stuff one's mouth to fill the lavatory bowl. Though these pleasures belong together. As the arousing parts and the dirty parts of the body are placed so closely together one can see how sex and eating belong together".*

*Georgina's glances wander repeatedly to the other table. Unexpectedly she gets up and hurries to the toilets. She does not stay long. He had followed her. He shows himself, and his interest, but leaves the room again quickly. Georgina turns round and about - a ballet of indecision. She hurries back to the dining room.*

*Glances of desire shuttle from table to table. Restlessly she hurries again to the loo. "I forgot my cigarette lighter". Newly blushing she meets him, shyly takes his hand and guides it demandingly to her breasts. The lover urges her into the pale white of the toilets and against a cubicle, starts to undress her. He discovers her black camisole and immaculate alabaster skin. He peppers her with greedy kisses, panting with lust.*

Scene from the film: "The Cook, The Thief, His Wife and Her Lover" directed by Peter Greenaway.

*A selection of fresh herbs will make any salad special, but lovage is an herb you can trust every time for its aphrodisiac effect.*

## Spring-in-your-Step Salad

*mixed salad leaves (iceberg lettuce, curly endive, rocket, lollo rosso, dandelion and young stinging nettles)*
*6 baby radishes*
*1 tbs. red wine vinegar*
*3 tbs. sunflower oil*
*pepper*
*1/2 clove garlic*
*fresh aromatic herbs (chervil, parsley, oregano, barnet, lovage)*
*to garnish: chives and cress*

**Wash and dry the salad leaves. Cut the top of the radishes into 'zigzag' patterns in concentric circles, and place them in a bowl of lukewarm water so that they open up into little roses. Prepare the dressing by combining the vinegar, oil, salt, pepper, the crushed garlic, and chopped herbs. Toss the salad leaves and divide them between the two serving plates, drizzle the dressing over the salad and sprinkle with chives and cress. Garnish with the radish 'roses'.**

*Courgette flowers are the ultimate erotic delicacy - a gem of a recipe from Italy.*

## Frisky Fried Courgette Flowers

*3 tbs. flour*
*1 tbs. white wine*
*5 tbs. cold water*
*10 courgette (or pumpkin) flowers*
*peanut oil for frying*

Mix the flour, wine and water together, and add some salt. Let the batter stand for around 30 minutes. Very carefully dip the flowers in cold water, only holding them by the stems. Place them on some kitchen paper and until they have completely dried. Take the flowers by the leaves that surround them and lightly press them together so that the flowers do not become swamped by the batter. Next, hold the flowers by the stem and dip them into the batter, and then fry them briefly in hot oil. Lay the flowers on a kitchen roll to absorb excess oil.

Variation: the flowers can be stuffed before frying. Carefully put half a finely chopped anchovy fillet and coarsely chopped mozzarella cheese inside the flowers, and hold by the stems and fry them.

*Because of their shape and their fast growth, in times gone by, mushrooms were known as the phalluses of the earth. Truffles and morels are highly thought of by aphrodisiac connoisseurs, but mushrooms definitely play their part as well.*

## Snugly Stuffed Mushrooms

*10 large flat mushrooms*
*75g shallots*
*butter*
*1 bunch parsley*
*thyme sprigs*
*black pepper*
*sweet paprika*
*a few tbs. white wine*

Clean the mushrooms, and remove the stems. Very finely dice all the stems along with two of the mushrooms. Remove the skin of the shallots and chop them finely. Heat 1 tbs. butter in a pan and fry the shallots until they are translucent and then add the chopped mushrooms. As the mushrooms fry, add as much butter as they need to absorb. Season with the chopped herbs, salt, pepper, paprika and cook over a medium heat, until any moisture has been absorbed. Fill the mushroom heads with the mixture, and place next to each other in a greased baking tin. Pour the wine over the mushrooms and bake in an oven preheated to 200°C for 25 minutes.

*'The roots and flesh of the artichoke, when eaten with salt, pepper opens the way for unchaste seeds.'*

P.A. Matthiolus, Italian doctor and teacher, 16th century.

## Artichokes with Quail

*2 artichokes*
*lemon juice*
*rocket*
*2 quails*
*pepper*
*butter*
*1 tbs. sherry vinegar*
*2 tbs. grape seed oil*

Remove the stems of the artichokes, also removing the leaves and fibres. Cut the artichokes into fine strips and blanch in boiling water which has had lemon juice added to it. After a minute or so, plunge into cold water, and dry the artichokes thoroughly. Clean the salad and drain well.

Clean the quails thoroughly and cut the meat from the top of the breastbone down to where the legs join. Separate and remove the halves of the breast meat and remove the bone, so that the legs are attached to the deboned breast meat. Season the meat with salt and pepper, and fry in hot butter until it is cooked pink (do not overcook the meat). Set aside so that the meat cools and then remove the legs from the breast meat.

Shortly before serving, prepare the artichokes and the salad by making up a dressing with the salt, pepper, oil and vinegar and drizzle it over the salad. Slice the quail breast in two, and serve with the legs on a bed of the salad.

*Rabbit and hare meat are great aphrodisiacs, on account of their prolific breeding habits.*

## Raring-to-go Rabbit Salad

*1 rabbit fillet*
*3 juniper berries*
*black pepper*
*butter*
*radiccio leaves*
*30g lamb's lettuce*
*50g mushrooms*
*25g smoked streaky bacon*
*1 tbs. olive oil*
*1/2 tsp. honey*
*2 tbs. apple vinegar*

Wash and dry the rabbit fillet, and rub the meat with black pepper and the juniper berries. Fry the rabbit quickly to seal the meat, and then season with salt. Reduce the heat and fry for ten minutes. Remove from the heat and set the meat aside.

While the rabbit is frying, wash and dry the salad and arrange the leaves on two plates. Clean and slice the mushrooms and add them to the meat in the frying pan. Remove the rabbit and mushrooms and keep warm.

Finely dice the bacon and fry it in the same oil that was used to cook the rabbit. Remove the bacon and reserve the cooking fat. Stir in the honey, remove from the stove and add the vinegar, salt, and pepper and drizzle the sauce over the salad. Slice the rabbit fillet and arrange the slices on the plates, next to or on top of the salad. Garnish with chives and the bacon cubes.

*'Asparagus is a favourite dish of the idler, because whenever it is eaten, it weakens the will.'* Adamus Lonicerus in 'The Book of Herbs' (1783)

## Asparagus and Pork Salad

*100g white asparagus*
*100g green asparagus*
*200g pork fillet*
*white pepper*
*1 tbs. vegetable oil*
*2 tbs. balsamic vinegar*
*3 tbs. olive oil*
*few sprigs of rosemary*
*2 sprigs of thyme*
*lemon balm*

Wash and peel the white asparagus and steam in a little salt water for 15-18 minutes. Peel the lower third of the green asparagus and steam for up to ten minutes in salted water. Drain the asparagus.

Wash the meat, dab it dry with a kitchen towel and coat in pepper. Fry the pork on a very high heat to seal it, and then reduce the heat and fry for 7 to 9 minutes - the meat should still be pink on the inside.

While the pork is frying, put the vinegar, olive oil, rosemary and the thyme leaves in a pan and heat slowly, stirring constantly.

Cut the pork into as thin slices as possible and dip both sides into the warm marinade. Serve with both kinds of asparagus and garnish the meat with lemon balm.

*Oysters are widely held to be the strongest aphrodisiac, perhaps because of their texture, but more likely because of their zinc content. In the past, sometimes even the shell was used in love potions, being powdered and included in a drink. King Ludwig IV is said to have presented his Spanish wife, the Infanta Maria Theresa with 400 oysters upon their wedding.*

## Orgasmic Oysters on Leaf Spinach with Champagne Sauce

*12 oysters*
*200g fresh leaf spinach*
*2 shallots*
*50g butter*
*125ml single cream*
*7 tbs. champagne*
*white pepper*
*grated nutmeg*
*cayenne pepper*
*1 tsp. lemon juice*
*1 tsp. finely chopped chives*

**Carefully open the oysters using an oyster knife, and prise the flesh from out of the shells. Reserve all the juices from the oysters and set aside. Wash the spinach and blanch in boiling water very quickly and then plunge the leaves into cold water, so that the leaves keep their colour. Finely chop one of the shallots and fry in butter until they are translucent, making sure it does not brown. Add the spinach and fry for a few seconds. For the sauce, take the other shallot, chop it finely and fry it in 10g butter until it is translucent, and then pour in the cream and cook on a high heat, until the cream has thickened. Add the champagne and cook briefly. Season with salt, pepper, nutmeg, cayenne pepper**

and lemon juice. Take the sauce off the heat and add the juices from the oysters, which should be sieved to remove sand or shell fragments.

Real oyster fans and would-be lovers should eat the oysters raw, but if preferred, the oysters can be placed in the hot sauce for up to 20 seconds and removed using a slotted spoon. Arrange the spinach on two plates, and lay the oysters on the bed of spinach. Stir the sauce and add cubes of the remaining butter, and allow them to melt into the sauce. Pour the sauce over the oysters and garnish with chives.

*Aphrodite rose out of the sea in a mussel shell, off the coast of Cyprus. In many cultures, the mussel is seen as a symbol of the vulva, and from ancient to modern times, mussels have kindled and aroused the ardour of lovers.*

## Mouth-Watering Mussels in a Riesling Sauce

*1kg mussels*
*1 carrot*
*1 stick celery*
*3-4cm leek*
*1 clove garlic*
*1 shallot*
*2 tbs. oil*
*pepper*
*125ml Riesling wine*
*1/2 bunch flat leaf parsley*
*crusty baguette*

Carefully sort the mussels; wash them under running water and remove their 'beards'. Discard any open mussels. Finely chop the carrot, celery, leek, garlic and shallot. Heat some oil in a saucepan and fry the garlic and shallot until they are translucent. Add the vegetables, salt and pepper and sweat them for a few minutes. Pour in the wine, add the mussels and cook in a covered saucepan for 4-5 minutes, regularly shaking the pot. The mussels are ready when the shells have opened. Discard any shells that have not opened. Garnish the mussels with chopped parsley and serve in deep bowls with a baguette.

*Ginger is known and used in many parts of the world, and it is renowned for its ability to arouse sexual interest.*

## Spicy Goose Breast with Melons and Fresh Ginger

*20g ginger root*
*1/2 melon*
*100g smoked goose breast*
*mint leaves*

Remove the skin of the ginger and cut into strips about 3cm, and place in hot, salted water ofr a few minutes. Take them out and leave to cool. Remove the seeds from the melon, remove the rind and cut into large but thin slices. Arrange the melons in a fan shape on the plate and top with the ginger. Cut the goose into thin slices, and serve it with the melon. Garnish with mint leaves.

*'The avocado arouses sexual passion. Ludwig IV called it 'la bonne poire' (the good pear) because it appeared to revive his declining libido'* Robert Hendrikson in 'Fools for Love' (1974)

## Avocado, Mussel and Caviar Salad

*2 shallots*
*2 tbs. olive oil*
*juice of 2 lemons*
*6-8 green peppercorns*
*4 large green-lipped mussels*
*1/2 tbs. chopped fresh basil*
*2 avocados*
*black pepper (slightly crushed)*
*2 tsp. red caviar*
*1 tbs. finely chopped chives*

Finely chop the shallots and mix them with the olive oil, three-quarters of the lemon juice, the basil and the peppercorns. Wash the mussels, and finely chop the main part of the mussel. Keep the pink part of the mussels intact. Marinate both parts of the mussels in the dressing, and cool for one hour.

Halve the avocados lengthways, remove the stone, and squeeze the lemon juice over the flesh to prevent the avocado from browning. Remove the avocado from its skin, keeping the skin in one piece. Keep two skins for later. Purée the avocado with the rest of the lemon juice. Season with salt and black pepper.

Remove the mussels from the marinade, and reserve two pink parts of the mussels for the garnish, mix into the avocado purée. Spoon the mixture into the avocado shells and garnish each with a pink part of the mussel.

*Apples and nuts are traditional symbols of female fertility, and it is said that celery works wonders for male potency.*

## Come-to-the-Crunch Celery Salad

*head of baby celery*
*200g cooking apples*
*lemon juice*
*50g walnut kernels*
*40g whipped cream*
*white pepper*
*sugar*
*40g mayonnaise*
*to garnish: salad leaves, cress, walnut kernels, baby tomatoes*

**Peel the apple and using a potato peeler, peel the strands off the sticks of celery. Cut them both into pieces approximately 2cm long. Squeeze lemon juice over the apple straight away to prevent them going brown. Chop the walnuts and add to the apple and celery.**

**For the dressing, combine the salt, pepper and a pinch of sugar along with the mayonnaise. Stir the salad into the dressing and place in the fridge to cool. Before serving, decorate with salad leaves, cress, walnuts and tomatoes.**

*Core, the daughter of Demeter was kidnapped by Hades, and was taken down into the depths of the earth, where she was fed pomegranate seeds. This caused her to be transformed from an innocent girl into both a woman and a lover.*

## Persephone's Liver Salad with Pomegranate Vinaigrette

*1 tbs. raisins*
*2-3 tbs. red wine*
*1 pomegranate*
*1 tbs. small capers*
*1 tsp. balsamic vinegar*
*1 tbs. red wine vinegar*
*pepper*
*1 tsp. liquid honey*
*1 tbs. olive oil*
*3 tbs. vegetable oil*
*60g iceberg lettuce*
*100g duck liver*
*2 tbs. concentrated stock*

**Pour the wine over the raisins, and leave covered for a couple of hours for the wine to soak in. Diagonally halve the pomegranate and remove the seeds. Add the seeds and capers to the raisins and mix well.**

**Mix up a salad sauce with the two kinds of vinegar, salt, pepper, honey, olive oil, and two tablespoons of vegetable oil and add it to the pomegranate mixture.**

**Wash and dry the salad, and break into bite-sized pieces.**

**Clean the liver and remove any fat and sinews and cut into pieces. Heat the rest of the vegetable oil and fry the liver over a**

very hot heat for a short time to seal in the juices. Remove from the heat and keep the liver warm.

Add the concentrated stock to the pan and reduce the sauce down to half the original volume. Soak the liver in the juices briefly before serving.

Toss the salad and dressing together in a basin, share the salad between the two plates and arrange the liver on top of the salad. Pour any remaining juices from the pan over the liver before serving.

*Figs are the crowning glory of any romantic meal - despite their appearance!*

## Beguiling Honeydew Melon, Parma Ham and Figs

*2 small honeydew melons*
*8 ripe figs*
*150g Parma ham*

Make sure that the melons are well chilled. Halve each melon and carefully remove the seeds, and then cut the melon lengthways into slices, and remove the skin. Arrange eight slices on each plate in a star formation. Remove the skin from the figs, place them in alternate spaces between the melon slices, and finally arrange the ham in the remaining spaces on the plate.

*Onions don't only make you cry; they also arouse passion. Together with stimulating cloves and strengthening ginger, you simply cannot fail!*

## Greek Style Onions

*350g medium sized onions*
*cloves*
*2 tbs. olive oil*
*1/2 tsp. sugar*
*3/4 glass red wine*
*juice of 1/2 lemon*
*1/2 tsp. ground ginger*
*1 tsp. capers*
*pepper*

Remove the skin from the onions and stick 4 cloves in each onion. Fry each of them in hot oil and sugar until they are golden brown. Add the wine, lemon juice, ginger and capers and season with salt and pepper. Cook over a low heat for 15 minutes.

*Shrimps in combination with certain spices can turn every night into a wedding night!*

## Ceylonese Wedding Cakes

*300g yellow lentils*
*150g finely chopped onions*
*200g shrimps*
*80g soaked raisins*
*3 tbs. finely chopped chillies*
*2 tbs. chopped almonds*
*3 tbs. flour*
*garam masala*
*cinnamon*
*saffron*
*ginger*
*chilli*
*oil for frying*

**Soak the lentils overnight, mash them slightly and cook until the lentils have turned into a mushy paste. Sweat the onions. Remove from the heat and add the shrimps, raisins, chillies, almonds, flour and lentils. Mix well and season with salt and the spices. Mould the mixture into 4 patties and fry in hot oil until both sides are golden brown.**

## SINFUL SOUPS

*"Those who have thoughts of producing children, with the delight and pleasure that accompanies the act, will require more semen. Their coitus will be more effective, if they, before they commence this business, prepare a vegetable soup with fresh bread and half raw egg white, so that it becomes milky. Before he takes a woman, he should eat this for three or four days each morning and evening before the meal. I don't believe there is anything better in this case."*

D. Agostino Lamponani from "Abate Cassinese", (1653).

*The witches of Thessaloniki and the wise women of India used to prescribe asparagus juice as a love potion. The Italian doctor, P.A. Matthiolus wrote: 'When asparagus is included in the diet, it causes men to have lustful longings and desires.'*

## Asparagus Soup

*250g white asparagus (not necessarily the best quality)*
*50g butter*
*5-6 tbs. cream*
*5-6 tbs. veal or chicken juices*
*pepper*
*1 tbs. whipped cream*
*chervil leaves*

**Wash and peel the asparagus. Cut off the heads and cut the stalks into pieces about 2-3cm long. Heat some butter and cook the asparagus for 8-10 minutes.**

**Take the asparagus heads out and put to one side. Add the cream and meat juices to the rest of the asparagus and cook through for a short amount of time. Purée finely in a mixer and season with salt and pepper.**

**Before serving, stir in the whipped cream; arrange the asparagus heads and the chervil leaves on top of the soup.**

## Merry Mussel Soup

*250g mussels*
*1 small onion*
*30g butter*
*250ml dry white wine*
*330 ml stock*
*black pepper*
*1 cup sour cream*
*12 mussels or 6 green-lipped mussels*
*1 tsp. lemon juice*
*grated nutmeg*
*1 egg yolk*
*1 bunch parsley*
*thyme*

Clean, blanch and finely chop the 250g mussels. Finely chop the onions and sweat in hot butter and the mussels and cook for 5 minutes. Add the stock and the wine, season with salt and pepper and simmer for 20 minutes. Pass through a sieve and add sour cream.

In the meantime, take the rest of the mussels and fry them in some butter and lemon juice for 10 minutes. Season with a pinch of nutmeg, salt and pepper.

Bring the soup to the boil, remove it from the stove and thicken with the egg yolk. Put half the mussels in each bowl, garnish with chopped herbs, and ladle the soup over them and serve immediately.

*Even as far back as 3500 BC, the Egyptians held the onion to be an aphrodisiac. Monks in the Middle Ages were forbidden to eat onions lest they gave in to temptation.*

## Aphrodisiac Onion Soup

*2 medium sized onions*
*1 tbs. melted butter*
*pepper*
*ground caraway seeds*
*1/2 tsp. herbes de provence (thyme, rosemary, tarragon, oregano, marjoram)*
*1 tbs. flour*
*350 ml meat stock*
*150 ml white wine*
*2 pieces white bread*
*50g grated gruyere or emmental cheese*

Slice the onions into thin rings and fry in the butter until they are golden brown. Season with salt, pepper, the herbs and a knife tip of caraway. Sieve the flour over the onions. Sweat the ingredients briefly and add the stock while stirring constantly so that lumps do not form. Add the wine and cook the soup over a low heat for 15 minutes.

Toast the bread under the grill, and spread the cheese on the top of each piece. Place the bread in fireproof soup bowls, and carefully pour the soup over the bread. Place the bowls under the grill until the cheese has melted, and serve immediately.

*According to the ancient Greeks, saffron stimulated female desire, and hastened the sexual development of young men.*

## Saffron Fish Soup

*250g fish fillets (pike, perch or halibut)*
*1 small kohl rabi*
*1 thin leek*
*1 shallot*
*1 clove garlic*
*20g butter*
*flour*
*500 ml fish stock*
*saffron*
*white pepper*
*lemon juice*
*2 tbs. double cream*
*1 tsp. finely chopped chives*

Wash the fish in cold water, and cut into pieces or bite-sized strips. Peel the kohl rabi and cut into thin narrow strips. Fry the diced shallots with the garlic (finely chopped) in the butter until the shallots are transparent. Add the vegetables and the flour and sweat for a few minutes, stirring often. Pour the stock into the pan while stirring the shallots with a wooden spoon, so the flour doesn't form lumps. Season with a knife tip of saffron, salt and pepper. Cook on a low heat for 6-8 minutes. Season the fish pieces with salt and pepper and squeeze lemon juice over them, and place them in the soup stock. Cook them for 2 minutes and then remove them, laying them in the two soup bowls. Stir in the double cream, briefly bring to the boil and pour the stock over the fish. Before serving, garnish with chives.

*Fish, leek, celery and basil - not a recipe for a chaste evening.*

## Sweet and Sour Fish Soup

*200g fish fillets (sole and tuna)*
*4 tomatoes*
*2 slices fresh pineapple*
*2 onions*
*1 leek*
*2 sticks celery*
*2 tbs. lemon juice or wine vinegar*
*125g fresh bean shoots*
*sugar*
*oil*
*2 tbs. Vietnamese fish sauce (nuoc mam)*
*pepper*
*1 fresh chilli*
*1 bunch basil*

Wash the fish and dice the fillets. Boil the tomatoes whole, and remove their skin and then cut them into quarters. Cut the onions into thin slices and cut the leek and celery into pieces that are about 2cm long. Bring half a litre of water to the boil. Add the onions, tomatoes, leek, pineapple and lemon juice and cook for 10 minutes. Add the fish, bean sprouts, salt, sugar, oil, fish sauce, pepper and the chopped chilli and cook for 5 minutes. Garnish with finely chopped basil and serve immediately.

*'Aniseed, ginger and coriander should succeed where other remedies have failed'*

Jacobus Theodorus Tabernaemontanus in 'The New and Comprehensive Herb Book' (1731)

## Geisha Soup

*60g pork fillet*
*1/2 tsp. rice or wheat flour*
*1 tsp. ground coriander*
*1 tsp. vegetable oil*
*sugar*
*ground black pepper*
*250g pak choy*
*melted butter*
*2 sticks fresh ginger*
*1 egg*
*star anise*

Cut the meat into wafer thin strips. Mix the flour, coriander, a pinch of sugar and some pepper and coat the strips of meat in the mixture. Chop the pak choy into chunks about 1 or 2cm thick.

Heat the butter in a pan, and fry the ginger and salt for half a minute. Add the pak choy, and immediately pour 500 ml water into the pan and cook over a low heat for 5 minutes. Take the soup from the stove and stir in the egg which has been thoroughly whisked as well as a little star anise.

*'He who loves crabs will be pinched by love' Danish saying*

## Catch-Me Crab Soup

*1 onion*
*500ml chicken broth*
*1 lobster stock cube*
*250g fresh crab meat (not including shell)*
*2 tbs. creme fraiche*
*pepper*
*fresh dill or parsley*

Finely chop the onion and place in the stock. Bring to a rolling boil and add the stock cube. As soon as it has dissolved, reduce the heat, so that the soup is simmering. Add the crab meat and creme fraiche, stir well, and leave to stand for 10 minutes. Season with salt and pepper. Do not reheat the soup before serving as the soup must not boil. Before serving, garnish with dill or parsley.

*'Without lemons, love would not blossom'*
Hugo Hertwig, German biologist in 'Healing Plants' (1964)

## Luscious Lemon Soup

*4 garlic cloves*
*2 tbs. olive oil*
*30g rice*
*500 ml vegetable stock*
*black pepper*
*1 clove*
*1 tsp. grated lemon peel*
*15 finely chopped mint leaves*
*3 egg yolks*
*1 tbs. lemon juice*

Finely chop the garlic and fry in hot oil, and add the rice grains and fry for 2-3 minutes, stirring frequently, so that the rice does not stick. Add the vegetable stock, pepper and clove, and simmer on a low heat for 40 minutes. Five minutes before the cooking time is up, add the lemon peel and mint leaves. Take the soup from the stove and remove the clove. In a large basin, beat the egg yolks thoroughly, and mix in the lemon juice. Pour the egg yolk mixture into the hot soup, stirring constantly - the egg yolk must not set or curdle. Season with salt.

*Exotic herbs make a meal more tasty, and they also stimulate the libido.*

## Mulligatawny Meat Soup

*300g finely chopped lean beef*
*butter*
*2 onions*
*1 red chilli pepper*
*1 tsp. coriander seeds*
*ground caraway*
*pepper*
*1 tbs. curry powder*
*sugar*
*3 cloves garlic*
*1 tin tomato puree*
*fresh coriander leaves*

Fry the beef in hot butter. Finely chop the onions and chilli. Lightly grind the coriander seeds in a mortar and pestle. Carefully fry the coriander seeds, ground caraway, chilli, pepper, curry powder, sugar and salt with the beef, taking care that the spices do not burn. Add the finely chopped garlic at the end, taking care that it does not burn. After a minute, add the tomato purée and 400 ml water, and simmer for 30 minutes.

*Regarding chilli: "One should never add more than more than twelve seeds to a dish, otherwise one will cause suffering, and people will be driven quite mad."*
Adamus Lonicerus in the Herb Book (1783)

## Pumpin' Pumpkin Soup

*2 cloves garlic*
*1 red chilli pepper*
*2 cups meat stock*
*peanut oil*
*1 onion*
*2 slices toast*
*250g pumpkin*
*80g fresh leaf spinach*

Using a pestle and mortar, grind the garlic and chilli into a paste. Empty the garlic and chilli into a dish and add the meat stock while stirring constantly. In a saucepan, heat the oil and fry the chopped onion until it is golden brown. Remove the crusts from the toast and fry in the oil, and pour in the meat stock. Finely chop the pumpkin and add to the soup and simmer for 10 minutes. Season with salt, and then liquidise in a blender. Pour the soup back into the saucepan and re-heat, add the leaf spinach and then simmer on a low heat for 5 minutes.

*A shot of Vermouth inspires ardour. This recipe is an energising idea from the Far East.*

## Naughty Nori Soup with Egg

*2 large sheets nori seaweed*
*500ml chicken stock*
*2 finely chopped spring onions*
*1/4 tsp. finely chopped ginger*
*1 tbs. vermouth*
*dash of sesame oil*
*2 eggs*

**Roast the seaweed very briefly in a dry pan, until it is turns a greenish colour. Crumble the sheets of nori and add to the chicken broth. Bring the stock to the boil and then reduce the heat, and add all the ingredients except for the egg. Whisk the eggs and pour into the soup. As soon as the soup has thickened, serve immediately.**

## 'Come to me' Courgette Soup

*2 medium-sized courgettes*
*2 medium-sized onions*
*500ml chicken or vegetable stock*
*125g natural yoghurt*
*black pepper*
*chives*

Cut the courgettes into sticks and the onions into thick slices. Bring the stock to the boil and add the courgettes and onion, and simmer until the courgettes can easily be pierced with a knife. Liquidise the vegetables and stock, add the yoghurt and season with salt and pepper. Garnish with chives. If the soup is to be served chilled, cool in the refrigerator for a few hours before serving.

## OCEANS OF LOVE

*"In France, we know that those who live almost exclusively on shell-fish and fish, which are mostly made up of water, are much more fiery in love than others. Indeed, we feel much more drawn towards love during Lent than at any other time of the year, not because of required abstinence, but because during this time we sustain ourselves on fish and herbs; nourishments which contain much water".*

**Nicolas Venette in "Paper on the Procreation of Humans" (1762).**

## Saucy Steamed Fish with Saffron

*500g fish (pike, carp, perch or any white fish)*
*1 tbs. fruit vinegar*
*1 onion*
*10 leaves basil*

*for the marinade:*
*1 onion*
*2 cloves garlic*
*1g saffron*
*1 tbs. Vietnamese fish sauce (nuoc mam)*

*for the sauce:*
*1 ginger root*
*1 clove garlic*
*pepper*
*1 chilli*
*2 tbs. Vietnamese fish sauce*

Scale and clean the fish thoroughly. Either use the fish whole or cut it into 3cm thick slices, and rub with vinegar and salt.

For the marinade, chop the onion very finely and crush the clove of garlic, and combine with the saffron and 1 tbs. of the fish sauce. Pour over the fish and leave to stand for 2 hours.

Heat some oil in a pan and fry a few slices of onion until they are brown but not burnt. Add 125ml water and then add the fish along with the marinade. Bring to the boil and simmer with the pan covered for 30 minutes, so that the fish steams. Five minutes before serving, throw in a portion of the finely chopped basil leaves.

For the sauce, peel the ginger and cut into very thin slices, and crush the clove of garlic. Add the pepper and chopped chilli, along with the Vietnamese fish sauce and pour into a sauce boat. Stand the sauce boat in the middle of a large plate. Arrange the fish on once side, and put the rest of the basil leaves on the other side. Serve with steamed rice.

## Steaming Catfish

*300g catfish cutlets*
*2 tbs. lemon or lime juice*
*white pepper*
*ground coriander*
*150ml fish stock*
*2 tbs. ice cold butter*

Wash the fish steaks and drizzle with lemon or lime juice. Season with salt, pepper, and coriander, and lay in a greased steamer.

In a saucepan, bring the fish stock to the boil, add the fish and put the lid on the pan. Steam for two minutes, turn the fish and steam for a further 3 minutes. Take the fish out and keep it warm.

Cut the butter into small cubes, and bit by bit, whisk the butter into the fish stock. Season, and serve with the fish. Serve with steamed broccoli or boiled new potatoes.

## Perfect Perch with Orange Sauce

*300g perch fillets*
*juice of one lemon*
*2 tbs. flour*
*50g butter*
*coarsely ground black pepper*
*juice of one orange*

Drizzle the lemon juice over the washed fillets. Leave the fish to stand in the fridge for 50 minutes.

Take the fish fillets out of the fridge and remove excess moisture and coat with the flour. Fry the fish fillets in hot butter until they are golden brown. Season with salt and a lot of black pepper, and add the orange juice. While it is cooking, baste the fish frequently with the butter in the pan. Serve with boiled new potatoes.

## Steamed Salmon in a Champagne Sabayon

*300g salmon fillet (in one piece)*
*2 tbs. lemon juice*
*white pepper*
*150ml fish stock*
*2 egg yolks*
*1 tsp. corn flour*
*75ml champagne (or white wine)*

Cut the salmon into two equal pieces and carefully remove the bones. Squeeze lemon juice over the fish and season with salt and pepper. Lay the salmon in a greased steaming basket and cover the saucepan. Steam for one minute, turn the fish and steam for a further 3 4 minutes. Take the fish out and keep warm.

Whisk the egg yolk, salt and pepper together in a basin, and place in a bain-marie. Beat in the fish stock and the champagne with a whip until it is a thick and foamy sauce. Season and serve the sabayon with salmon. Serve with a combination of long grain and wild rice.

## Skewered King Prawns

*10 raw king prawns*
*2 cloves garlic*
*3 tbs. olive oil*
*black pepper*
*cayenne pepper*
*1 tsp. finely ground oregano*
*1/2 lemon and the rind*

Wash the prawns. Using kitchen scissors, cut the entire length of the top of each prawn, and remove the vein and guts. Whisk the crushed garlic together with the oil, salt and herbs and spices. Mix in the zest of the lemon and some lemon juice. Marinate the prawns in the fridge for 3-4 hours. Put the prawns on skewers and grill for 6 minutes, turning halfway through cooking.

Serve with garlic bread.

## Trout with Capers and Sage

*2 medium sized trout*
*juice of 1 lemon*
*2 tbs. flour*
*50g butter*
*4 sage leaves*
*1 tbs. capers*
*50 ml white wine*

Wash the fish, and dry it thoroughly. Rub salt into the trout and drizzle with lemon juice. Leave to stand for 1 hour in the fridge.

Dry the fish using kitchen paper and coat with flour. Heat the butter in a pan and fry the trout with the sage leaves until it is golden brown. Shake the pan occasionally, so that the fish does not stick. Turn the fish and spread the capers over the fillets. Squeeze more lemon juice onto the fish and add the wine. Baste the fish with the butter and wine mixture so that it does not dry out while cooking. Remove from the stove and keep covered for 2 minutes so that the aroma of the capers can fully penetrate the fish. Serve immediately with new boiled potatoes.

## Scrumptious Squid and Vegetables

*1/2 bunch parsley*
*1 clove garlic*
*1 stick pepperoni*
*3 tbs. olive oil*
*100ml red wine*
*2 large tomatoes*
*400g fresh or deep frozen squid*
*150g mangold or beet leaves (pre-cooked and pressed dry)*
*lemon juice*

Crush the garlic and chop the parsley, and mix the two together. Fry half the mixture with the pepperoni in oil, and add the wine. Peel the tomatoes, pierce all over with a fork and add these to the pan.

Clean and gut the squid and cut into rings. Add them to the cooking mixture and cook for 1 hour. About 40 minutes into the cooking-time, add the leavse and some salt. When the hour is up, add the rest of the garlic and parsley mixture and season with lemon juice. Serve with polenta or bread.

## Cupid's Calamari

*1 bread roll (one day old)*
*100 ml milk*
*300g calamari*
*1/2 lemon (not squeezed)*
*80g mortadella ham*
*1 clove garlic*
*1 egg*
*1 egg yolk*
*1 bunch parsley*
*pepper*
*4 tbs. olive oil*
*100g tomatoes*
*50 petit pois*
*3-4 tbs. white wine*

Break up the bread roll into small pieces, and soak in the milk. Remove the ink sac and the eyes from the calamari and wash them thoroughly. Cook the calamari in boiling, salted water, along with slices of lemon for 20 minutes. Cut the tentacles off the squid, and finely chop them, and also finely chop the mortadella ham to a similar size. Mix the following ingredients together thoroughly: crushed garlic, egg, egg yolk, chopped parsley and the bread roll (squeeze the excess milk out first) and season with salt and black pepper.

Fill the squid tubes with the stuffing and sew up the opening with cooking thread. Lay the squid tubes in a greased heat-proof dish and drizzle with oil and bake in a preheated oven for about 20-30 minutes at 180°C. Halfway through cooking, add the white wine to form a sauce which can be poured over the stuffed calamari before serving. Serve with a risotto.

## Fillet of Steamed Fish in Green Sauce

*1 head celery*
*1 carrot*
*1 cream*
*125ml full fat cream cheese*
*1 tbs. chopped parsley*
*1 tsp. tarragon*
*2 shallots*
*250g fish bones or fish heads (fresh or cooked)*
*400g fish fillets (perch, flounder or other white fish)*
*pepper*
*1 tsp. Pernod*

Using a potato peeler, remove the fibres from the celery and the carrot and cut into fine strips. Finely chop the leek. Bring the vegetables to the boil. Puree the cream cheese with the parsley, tarragon and a third of the chopped shallots. Put the fish bones, fish heads, vegetables and the rest of the chopped shallots in a saucepan and fill with 2cm of water. Lay the fish fillets in a steamer. Put the steamer containing the fish in the saucepan, cover and cook for 2-3 minutes.

Put 3 tbs. of the liquid used to steam in a pan and reduce over a high heat to 1 tsp. Add the herb and cheese mixture and cook until the sauce has thickened. Season with salt and pepper and add Pernod according to taste.

Arrange the fillets on a warmed plate and serve the sauce separately.

## Salmon Pasta Indulgence

*300g salmon fillets or steaks*
*1 shallot*
*butter for frying*
*200ml cream*
*freshly ground black pepper*
*300g fresh tagliatelle*

Remove the skin, and carefully fillet the salmon and coarsely chop into bite-sized pieces. Finely chop the shallot and fry in butter until golden brown. Pour in the cream, add the salmon, and cook over a medium heat for about 3-4 minutes.

Meanwhile, cook the tagliatelle until it is 'al dente' (fresh pasta only needs a few minutes), and serve a portion into each bowl. Pour the salmon sauce over the tagliatelle and season with a little freshly ground black pepper before serving.

## Cheeky Charr in White Wine Sauce

*250ml white wine*
*50g carrots (cut into thin strips)*
*1 onion*
*1/2 tsp. chopped thyme*
*parsley*
*1 bay leaf*
*1/2 tsp. peppercorns*
*2 charr (approx. 400g)*

In a frying pan, cook the following ingredients in butter for 15 minutes: wine, finely chopped onion, thyme, some parsley, bay leaf, 1 tsp. salt and pepper. Remove from the heat and leave to cool for 3-4 minutes. Salt the insides of the fish, and lay the fish in the sauce and leave covered for 7-9 minutes. Remove the fish and serve on a pre-warmed plate. Serve with the wine sauce and also with boiled new potatoes.

## LOVE BIRDS

*In 414BC, the Greek poet Aristophanes mentioned in his comedy "The Birds", an episode from ancient mythology in which the God of Love, Amor, hatched out of a silver egg and so setting the act of love in motion. In all cultures, eggs symbolise fertility and vitality. It is fascinating to see how many eggs a chicken lays in its lifetime, and also somehow embarrassing to see how the cockerel rules the roost with such potency. This is why the ancient Greeks put poultry at the top of the menus celebrating Aphrodite the Goddess of Love. During the Renaissance, most birds were destined to a short life. Aristotle noted that a sparrow "in one hour coupled eighty three times", and as a result, all sorts of mixtures of sparrow brain and other aphrodisiac additions were widely used. Many women had a particular craving for testicles and combs of young cockerels, in the belief that it would raise their enjoyment, and this belief led to worrying massacres of the poultry population. The delicacies would be prepared in artfully seasoned pasties, as Pierre de Bourdeille, Sier de Brantome (French writer, 1540-1614) was known to report: "Of these finely mixed pasties, small cockerels, artichoke hearts, truffles or other inflaming delicacies many ladies make frequent use. When they eat these and fish around in the food, they dip their fork into it and take out either an artichoke, a truffle, a pistachio nut or a comb of a cockerel and put it into their mouth; to which they say with a sad expression say: "Miss!" Should they, however, catch an agreeable organ of a cockerel and get their teeth into it, they say jubilantly: "Hit!"*

## Delectable Duck Breast With Blood Orange Butter

*4 blood oranges (whole)*
*1 tsp. sugar*
*300ml concentrated duck gravy*
*30ml Campari Bitter*
*100g butter*
*1 tbs. green peppercorns*
*2 small duck breasts*
*white pepper*

Wash three of the blood oranges, grate the orange peel, and squeeze the oranges and reserve the juice. Take 300ml of the juice, the zest, sugar and duck gravy and cook on a high heat and reduce to a syrup. Add the Campari, cook further, and strain through a sieve. With a whisk, beat in the butter, add the peppercorns, and keep the sauce warm.

Wash the fourth orange thoroughly. Using a zester, peel the zest of the orange in strips, and cut into 2-3cm long pieces, and blanch in hot water to soften them. Segment the orange, removing the skin and membranes between the segments. Reserve any juice resulting from segmenting the orange, and warm the orange pieces in a pan with these juices.

Season the duck breasts with salt and pepper, and score the skin in a diamond pattern, without piercing the meat. Fry the breast on the skin side first, so that the excess fat melts, and then fry the other side briefly until it is cooked pink (the duck should not be overcooked). Allow the duck to relax for 5 minutes before serving and then cut diagonally into strips, and garnish with the orange butter, orange segments and zest.

Serve with mange tout beans, angel hair pasta, or potato gratin.

## 'Coconutty About You' Chicken

*1kg whole chicken*
*500ml coconut milk*
*4 cloves garlic*
*1 tbs. roasted peanuts*
*1 tbs. caraway seeds*
*1 tbs. ground coriander*
*4 peppercorns*
*1 tsp. grated lemon rind*
*1 tbs. Vietnamese fish sauce (nuoc mam)*
*2 tsp. chilli*
*2 tbs. soy sauce*
*1 tbs. shrimp paste*
*1 tsp. sugar*

Wash the chicken, dry and place in a saucepan. Pour the coconut milk over the chicken, add a little salt and cook, covered for 1 hour and 10 minutes. Take the chicken out of the saucepan and remove the chicken from the bones and keep warm. Return the pan to the heat and reduce the cooking juices to half the original volume. Blend the following in a liquidiser: garlic, peanuts, caraway, coriander and pepper. Stir in the remaining ingredients into the blended mixture, and add to the sauce. Cook until the sauce is thick and creamy and then season it with salt. Place the warm chicken on the plates and pour on the sauce. Serve with saffron rice.

## Bronzed Chicken Breast in Lime Sauce

*2-3 limes*
*1 tbs. sugar*
*250ml chicken stock*
*150ml single cream*
*2 chicken breasts (including the skin and bone)*
*white pepper*
*2 tbs. butter*
*lemon balm*

Pre-heat the oven to 250 °C. Wash the limes and grate about 1 tsp. zest. Using a zester, peel off the rest of the green rind and cut into small pieces. Squeeze the juice from the limes and cook together with the grated rind, sugar and stock until the sauce is syrupy in consistency. Add the cream, and reduce to half the volume. Blanch the strips of lemon zest in hot water for a couple of minutes. Put them in the sauce shortly before serving. Season the chicken breasts with salt and pepper and put 1 tbs. butter in a baking tin and lay the chicken breasts on top, and bake in the oven, turning them frequently for 12 minutes, until they are golden brown but yet still moist inside. Remove the bones and keep the chicken warm.

Make the lemon sauce in the baking tin; place it on the stove and bring the juices to the boil and skim off any scum that develops while boiling. Pass through a fine sieve and work in the rest of the butter and add some salt if necessary. Cut the meat diagonally into strips. Arrange the chicken on the plate and pour the lime sauce over the chicken pieces, and garnish with the lemon balm. Serve with pasta.

## Spanish Saffron Chicken

*1 chicken (or 1 kg chicken quarters)*
*white pepper*
*2 tbs. olive oil*
*100g cured ham (Serrano or Parma ham)*
*1 clove garlic*
*1/2g saffron strands*
*1 sprig parsley*
*1 tbs. flour*
*10 ml white wine*
*400 ml chicken stock*
*grated nutmeg*
*200g fresh peas*
*2 hard-boiled eggs*
*2 slices bread*
*1/2 tbs. butter*

Wash the chicken and quarter it, separating the thighs and drumsticks. Season with salt and pepper and fry in oil.

Slice the ham into thin strips, add them to the pan and fry with the chicken for 1-2 minutes. Crush the garlic and add it to the frying pan, along with the saffron and parsley. Dust with flour and allow the flour time to absorb excess juices. Add the wine and the stock and simmer on a medium heat until the chicken is done.

Take the chicken pieces out of the sauce and keep warm. Reduce the sauce to half its volume and season with the nutmeg. Meanwhile, blanch the peas in hot water, and rinse off with cold water so that they keep their colour. Halve the hard-boiled eggs and force the egg yolks through a sieve and mix them into the sauce. Sieve the sauce and add the peas and allow them to warm through in the sauce, and finally pour over the chicken pieces.

Cut the pieces of toast into triangles, butter and toast them under the grill. Chop the egg whites up and sprinkle them over the saffron chicken. Garnish with the bread. Serve while very hot and serve rice as a side dish.

## Tender Chicken in Turmeric Sauce

*2 large chicken thighs (each weighing 250g)*
*white pepper*
*1 tbs. flour*
*butter*
*medium sized banana*
*1 tsp. chopped pistachios*

*for the sauce:*
*1 tbs. finely chopped onion*
*1/2 small cooking apple*
*1/2 tsp. paprika*
*1 tsp. turmeric powder*
*5 tbs. white port*
*300ml chicken gravy*
*200ml chicken stock*
*1 tsp. flour-butter (soft butter with flour kneaded into it)*
*200ml cream*
*1 tsp. honey*
*1 tbs. mango chutney*

Wash the chicken and tie the pieces together so that the top of the thigh lies on the lower thigh. Season with salt and pepper and coat in flour. Fry the pieces in butter until they are golden brown. Take the chicken out of the pan and drain the excess fat well. Pour the butter out of the pan.

For the sauce, add fresh butter to the frying pan and fry the onions until they are golden brown. Peel the apple, remove the core, finely chop half of it and add to the onions. Fry briefly before removing the pan from the heat. Add the paprika and turmeric and stir thoroughly. Bring to the boil and add the chicken, reduce the heat and simmer.

Take the cooked thighs out of the pan and keep warm, allowing the meat to relax for 10 minutes. Bring the sauce to the boil and carefully remove the fat and reduce. Stir the flour-butter into the sauce, and allow it to thicken, add the cream and reduce until the sauce is thick and creamy. Add the honey, salt and pepper and sieve the sauce. Remove the strings from the chicken and add to the sauce, along with the chutney and bring to the boil again.

Peel the banana and cut into slices lengthways, and fry in butter. Arrange the chicken and sauce on a pre-warmed plate and place the bananas on the side of the chicken and garnish with the chopped pistachios. Serve with buttery rice.

## Chicken Crepes Madeira

*For the crepes:*
*50g white flour*
*125ml milk*
*2 eggs*
*sugar*
*butter*
*for the filling:*
*150g stewing chicken*
*80g finely chopped chicken liver pepper*
*4 tbs. Madeira*
*100ml poultry stock*
*10ml single cream*
*1 tsp. finely chopped marjoram and thyme*
*1 tbs. chopped parsley*

For the crepe batter, place the flour in a glass dish and whisk the milk until there are no lumps. Work in the eggs, a pinch of salt, and sugar, as well as 1 tbs. melted butter, whisking the batter well. Leave to stand for 1-2 hours in the refrigerator. Then, using a small, well-buttered pan, make four crepes, lay them on top of each other, and keep them warm.

For the stuffing, heat the butter in a pan. Salt and pepper the chicken and the liver, and fry on a high heat. Take the meat out, and keep it warm. Pour the remaining butter out of the pan, pour the Madeira into the pan and add the stock. Reduce the sauce until it is quite thick in consistency. Add the cream, and cook until the sauce thickens once more. Season with the herbs, and add the chicken and liver to warm up again. Remove the crepes from the oven, share out the filling between the crepes, and roll up. Lay in a buttered, fireproof dish and warm in an oven and serve immediately.

## ANIMAL LUST

*For Thomas Aquinas the longing for meat was a mortal sin of both gluttony and pleasure. Accordingly, many servants of God banned meat from their kitchens. Many gourmets, on the other hand, did not want to forego meat. Apart from the usual lamb, veal and pork, roasted or simmered bone marrow could be found, as well as, of course their sexual parts, which were accompanied by fantastic promises: "Of great effectiveness is the sexual organ of a bull (especially when in rut). If one dries it, pulverises it and dissolves the powder in an egg, it has a wonderful effect".*

From Marinello, Italian doctor from the Renaissance period.

## Cognac Mutton Chops

*6 mutton chops (2cm thick)*
*6 anchovy fillets*
*6 rashers streaky bacon*
*butter*
*4 medium sized onions*
*2 cloves garlic*
*1/2 bunch parsley*
*1 bay leaf*
*basil*
*3-4 cloves*
*12 coriander seeds*
*2 tbs. good cognac*
*2 tbs. stock*
*pepper*

Secure an anchovy fillet and rasher of bacon to each cutlet with a toothpick. Melt the butter in a pan; sweat the finely chopped onions until they are translucent and fry the cutlets. Add the crushed garlic, chopped parsley, bay leaf, some basil, the cloves and coriander seeds. Add the cognac and stock. Season with salt and pepper and cook for 20 minutes.

Arrange the cutlets on the plate and pour the sauce over the meat. Serve with rice.

## Lemony Veal with Spring Vegetables

*8 small baby artichokes*
*juice of half a lemon*
*1 bunch spring onions*
*4 thin veal cutlets*
*pepper*
*olive oil*
*butter*

Wash the artichokes, remove the hearts and rub them immediately with lemon juice. Simmer them in boiling salted water for 15 minutes. Steam the spring onions in salted water for 4 minutes and drain well.

Using a tenderiser or a rolling pin, lightly beat the schnitzels and season them with salt and pepper. Put both the oil and butter in a frying pan and heat until the butter is foamy. Fry the schnitzels on one side for one minute each. Add some more butter and some lemon juice, raise the heat and turn the schnitzel again. Arrange the schnitzels on a pre-warmed plate and serve with the vegetables.

## Pork Roll-Over

*4 thin pork cutlets (each weighing approx. 60g)*
*pepper*
*1 clove garlic*
*100g fresh spinach*
*150g button mushrooms*
*1 onion*
*50g butter*
*grated nutmeg*
*150g raw sausage meat*
*125ml white wine*
*125ml cream*
*1 tbs. finely chopped parsley*
*toothpicks*

Wash the meat in cold water. Season with salt, pepper and a crushed clove of garlic. Blanch the spinach in boiling water for 1 minute, rinse in cold water and drain well. Clean the mushroom and cut into thin slices. Finely dice the onion, and fry in some butter until the onion turns translucent. Add the spinach and steam for 3 minutes. Season with salt, pepper and nutmeg. Spread the spinach mixture over each cutlet, and spread the sausage meat over the spinach. Roll each piece of meat up, and secure with a toothpick and season.

Heat the rest of the butter and fry the pork rolls on all sides. Add the mushrooms, cook for a couple of minutes and then pour some wine over the meat. Finally, add the cream and cook over a low heat for 20 minutes.

Take the rolls out of the pan, remove the toothpicks and keep warm. Cook the sauce, adding pepper and parsley until it is creamy. Serve the rolls with the sauce and rice or noodles.

## Plummy Pork Fillets

*2 lean pork cutlets or 4 pork fillets*
*pepper*
*thyme*
*2 half plums (fresh or tinned)*
*250ml marsala or white wine*
*butter*
*1 chopped shallot*
*2 tsp. redcurrants*
*2 tbs. meat stock*
*cayenne pepper*
*1 tbs. green peppercorns (ground)*

Season the meat with the pepper and the thyme. Slice the plums into pieces and put with the marsala in a bowl to marinate. Fry the meat in the butter until it is golden brown and season it with salt. Remove the excess fat from the frying pan before adding the shallots, frying them briefly and pouring in half of the marsala. Steam for 20 minutes. Take the meat out of the pan and keep warm. Sieve the cooking juices and pour in the rest of the marsala. Turn the heat up high and reduce the liquid to half its volume. Add the redcurrants and the meat stock, cook for a couple of minutes and season with a couple of pinches of cayenne pepper. Finally, whisk a few pieces of butter into the sauce with a whisk. Warm the plum slices in the marsala and decorate the meat with the fruit. Ladle the sauce over the meat and serve with rice.

## Bordeaux Steak

*2 shallots or 1 onion*
*butter*
*125ml stock*
*2 large marrow bones (if available)*
*250ml red bordeaux wine*
*2 entrecôte steaks (150g each)*
*1 tbs. oil*
*3 tbs. meat juices*
*pepper*
*parsley*

Finely chop one of the shallots and fry in 2 tbs. butter, turning and stirring them regularly. In a separate pan, bring the stock to a boil and add the marrow bones. Remove the pan from the heat, and leave the bones to stand for a while. Keep the stock warm, and ensure that the marrow remains pink and does not overcook. Meanwhile, chop the other shallot. Pour the red wine into a pan and add the shallot and cook over a high heat, reducing the volume of the liquid to half. Lightly brush the steaks in oil and either grill or fry them as long as you wish, depending on whether you like your meat rare or well done. Add the rest of the wine to the reduced liquid, and reduce it once more to half the volume.

Season with meat with salt and pepper and place the steaks on a pre-warmed plate. Remove the marrow from the bones and chop it finely, and place half on each steak along with the chopped shallots. Whip some butter into the sauce until the sauce is slightly creamy in texture, season with salt and pepper and pour over the steaks. Garnish with parsley, and serve the steaks with steamed vegetables, rice or even a baguette.

## Fillet Steak Roquefort

*1 ripe pear*
*125ml red wine*
*2 fillet steaks (each weighing 200g)*
*50g roquefort cheese*
*2 tbs. butter*
*black pepper*
*mint leaves*
*toothpicks*

Peel the pear, halve it lengthways and remove the core. Poach it for a few minutes in the wine. Put the pear aside.

Wash the steaks in cold water and dab them dry with a kitchen roll, and in the side of the steak, cut a slit so that a pocket is formed in the middle of the meat for the stuffing. Remove the rind from the cheese, and cut into medium sized chunks and fill the pockets of the steak with roquefort. Secure the stuffing using toothpicks. Fry the steaks in the melted butter on both sides for 2-3 minutes and pepper both sides. Remove the steaks from the pan, season them with salt and lay them on a warm plate. Cover with tin foil and keep warm.

Next, cut the pear halves into a fan: cut into the pear to form thin slices, but do not cut all the way through. Place each fan onto a warmed plate, spreading the fruit out into a fan shape. Garnish the pear with mint leaves. Place the steaks on the plate and serve with bread or potato croquettes. The steak can also be served with a red wine sauce, with the wine that was used to poach the pear.

## Sexy Italian Saltimbocca

*2-4 thin veal cutlets*
*pepper*
*4 slices of Parma ham*
*4 sage leaves*
*2 tbs. butter*
*1 knife tip of meat extract*
*toothpicks*

Wash the cutlets, dab them dry and pepper them. Top each cutlet with a slice of ham and a sage leaf, and secure with a toothpick. Fry both sides in butter, and then put aside and keep warm. Add half a glass of water to the cooking juices and add the meat extract and cook. Season (if necessary) with salt.

Put the saltimbocca on the plates and pour the sauce over them. Serve with mashed potato, risotto or steamed vegetables.

## Moist Veal in Herb Sauce

*500g veal*
*2 tbs. butter*
*pepper*
*4 tbs. oil*
*1 tbs. vinegar*
*2 hard-boiled eggs*
*4 tbs. fresh chopped herbs (parsley, sage, mint, chives)*

Fry the meat in butter, turning the pieces so that all sides are sealed to keep the moisture in. Season with salt and pepper and fry for 45 minutes, basting frequently. Remove the meat from the pan and leave it to 'relax' for a few minutes. Cut thin slices into the meat, but do not cut all the way through so that the meat does not fall apart.

Combine the oil, vinegar, herbs, salt and pepper to form a sauce. Pour the sauce frequently over the veal, so that it can penetrate the incisions and reach the heart of the meat.

Serve lukewarm with bread.

## Beef Bourguignon

*50g bacon*
*500g beef fillet*
*2 tbs. butter*
*pepper*
*1 carrot*
*1 onion*
*1 bay leaf*
*1 clove*
*1 celery stick*
*150 ml white wine*
*2 tbs. cream*
*1/2 tsp. corn flour*

Preheat the oven to 200 degrees C. Cut the bacon into strips about 3mm wide and 3cm long and wrap the beef with the bacon to form a skin around it, securing the bacon with a toothpick. Fry the fillet very briefly in hot butter to seal it, and season with salt and pepper. Stick the clove into the onion, and add it to the pan, along with the carrot, which has been cut lengthways in half, and the bay leaf. Pour the wine over the meat and bake for 20 minutes, basting the meat frequently so that it does not dry out. The meat should still be pink on the inside after 20 minutes.

Place the fillet on a heated plate, and add some water to the cooking juices, place the roasting tin on the stove and bring the water to a boil. Thicken the sauce with cream and stir in the corn flour. Pour the sauce over the meat, and carve it at the table. Serve with steamed baby vegetables and sauteed potatoes.

## Spareribs Aflame

*1kg spare ribs*
*4 tbs. soy sauce*
*4 tbs. oil*
*2 tbs. tomato ketchup*
*pepper*
*3 tbs. apricot jam*
*1 piece of ginger (walnut sized)*
*1 clove garlic*

Wash the spare ribs, dry and carefully separate the ribs with a sharp knife. Combine the soy sauce, oil, ketchup, pepper and jam. Peel the ginger and chop very finely, crush the garlic and mix both into the marinade. Thoroughly brush the spare ribs with the marinade and leave for at least two hours in the fridge. Grill the spare ribs for 20-30 minutes, turning and basting them frequently.

## Chilli Con Carne

*100g kidney beans or butter beans*
*150g pork fillet*
*1 onion*
*2 cloves garlic*
*1 tbs. olive oil*
*1 small tin peeled plum tomatoes*
*1 carrot*
*1 stick celery*
*1 green pepper (capsicum)*
*150g beef mince*
*125ml red wine*
*200ml meat stock*
*1/2 tsp. chopped thyme*
*1/2 tsp. chilli powder or 1-2 red chilli peppers*
*2 tbs. tomato puree (concentrated)*
*black pepper*

Soak the beans overnight to soften them. Finely dice the pork and onion and finely chop the garlic. Heat some oil in a saucepan and carefully fry the onion and garlic until they are golden brown, taking care not to burn the garlic. Add the pieces of meat and fry them, Add the tomatoes and their juices, cover the pan and cook over a low heat for 15 minutes. Peel the carrot and celery and finely dice, and remove the seeds from the green pepper and finely chop. Add the mince and stir well, and then add the vegetables and the soaked beans. Add the wine and stick and season with the thyme, chilli and tomato puree.

Cook on a low heat for 1 hour, or until the beans are soft, stirring frequently. If there is too much liquid in the chilli, remove the lid for the last 15 minutes. Before serving, season with salt and black pepper and serve with bread.

## Pleased-to-Meat-You Curry

*500g lamb shoulder (deboned)*
*1 onion*
*2 cloves garlic*
*40g butter*
*1 tsp. chilli powder or 1 chilli pepper*
*2 tsp. pepper*
*1 tsp. ground caraway*
*2 tsp. ground coriander*
*1 tsp. turmeric powder*
*2 small ripe tomatoes*
*juice of 1 lemon*
*300ml meat stock*
*2 tsp. garam masala*

Wash the meat, dab it dry with kitchen paper and remove excess fat and any fibres attached to the meat. Dice the meat into pieces about 2.5cm cubed. Finely chop the onion and garlic and fry in butter until they are golden brown in colour. Add the chilli, pepper, caraway, coriander and turmeric, and fry, taking care not to burn the spices. Quarter the tomatoes and add them to the pan. When the tomatoes are cooked, add the meat with some lemon juice and salt. Heat the stock and add it to the meat. Cook over a low heat for 45 minutes, stirring often. Finally, add the garam masala and cook for a further 10 minutes. Serve with rice.

## GAME FOR GAME

*For difficult cases, the student of magic, Caterina da Forli, recommended in her secret book of recipes:*

*"Take the testicles of a deer, or the tip of the brush of a fox as well as the testicles, as these inflame the desire of a woman. Also, if the rod of a man is rubbed with the gall of a boar or wild pig this at once provokes desirable lust in women."*

## Rack of Hare Caressed with Calvados

*1 hare rack (500g)*
*125ml white wine*
*1/2 onion*
*1 bay leaf*
*1/2 tsp. oregano*
*black pepper*
*1 tbs. butter*
*grated nutmeg*
*3 tbs. Calvados*
*4 tbs. apple wine*
*125ml game stock*
*50 ml cream*
*cayenne pepper*

Carefully remove the fillets from the rack. Put the following ingredients in a saucepan and bring them to the boil: white wine, coarsely chopped onion, bay leaf, oregano and 1/4 tsp. pepper. Lay the rack and the fillets in a bowl and pour the liquid over them and marinate in the fridge for 12 hours. Remove the rack and fillets from the marinade and fry in butter until they are golden in colour. Take the fillets out of the pan. Season the rack of meat with salt, pepper and nutmeg, cover the pan and cook for a further 15 minutes over a low heat. Pour the Calvados over the meat and flambé, to remove the excess alcohol. Remove the rack and keep warm. Add the apple wine and game stock, cream and a pinch of cayenne pepper and cook briefly until the sauce has thickened slightly.

Serve the meat and the sauce separately.

## Wild Boar with Baby Onions

*500g wild boar fillets*
*pepper*
*5 tbs. oil*
*2 onions*
*3 tbs. tomato puree*
*300ml red wine*
*100ml game stock*
*8 juniper berries*
*15 baby onions*
*4 slices streaky bacon*

Wash the meat, dab it dry with a kitchen towel and dice it into pieces about 3cm long. Season with salt and pepper. Heat the oil and fry the meat, turning it regularly. Finely dice the 2 onions and fry them until they are translucent. Stir in the tomato purée, pour in the wine and stock and the crushed juniper berries. Cook on a low heat for 45 minutes. In the last 10 minutes, add the baby onions. Season with salt and pepper. Cut the bacon into thin strips and fry them in a pan separately until they are crispy and sprinkle them over the ragout.

Serve with dumplings and red cabbage.

## Venison and Celery Sensation

*4 venison fillets*
*1/4 tsp. marjoram*
*pepper*
*5 potatoes*
*150g celery*
*2 tbs. lemon juice*
*2 tbs. butter*
*1 cooking apple*
*125ml white wine*
*1 tbs. cognac*
*100ml game stock*
*150ml cream*
*2 tbs. cranberries*

Wash the meat in cold water, dry it thoroughly and season both sides with marjoram and pepper. Leave for 15 minutes. Peel the potatoes, slice into pieces and boil them in salted water until they are ready. After peeling the celery, dribble the lemon juice over the stalks, finely dice and cook in salted water for 10 minutes until they are soft. Reserve the liquid they were cooked in. Now fry the celery in 1 tbs. butter for 3-4 minutes, until all excess moisture has evaporated. Purée the potatoes and the celery.

Peel the apple and cut it in half and boil it in 100ml water and 100ml white wine and the rest of the lemon juice until it is parboiled. Fry the venison until it is golden in colour and lightly salt the meat. Place on a warmed plate and keep warm. Add the cognac and the rest of the white wine to the cooking juices and add the stock and bring to the boil. Mix in 100ml of the cream and add half the berries.

Combine the rest of the cream with 1 tbs. of the celery water in a small pan, bring to the boil. Add the celery and potato puree and mix in with the cream in the pan. Warm the puree and add salt and 1/2 tbs. butter.

Stuff the apple halves with the rest of the berries. Pour the sauce over the venison, and serve with the mashed potatoes and celery and the apple halves.

## Venison Steak Bliss

*400g venison steaks*
*4 slices streaky smoked bacon*
*2 tbs. oil*
*1 tbs. mixed wild herbs*
*toothpicks*

Remove any fibres and excess fat from the meat, and cut into tournedos about 3-4cm thick. Wrap the bacon around the sides and secure with toothpicks. Sprinkle a little oil on both sides of the meat and coat them in the wild herbs, cover them and leave to marinate in the fridge for one hour.

Heat some oil in a pan and seal both sides of the meat over a high heat for 2 minutes on each side. Reduce the heat and fry for another 5 minutes. Serve immediately.

The steaks can be served with pasta, noodles or wild mushrooms.

## Venison Adorned with Figs and Grapes

*500g rack of venison*
*black pepper*
*sweet paprika*
*butter*
*3 tbs. game juices*
*3 tbs. red wine*
*4 fresh figs*
*100g green grapes*
*100g red grapes*

Wash the meat, dry thoroughly and season with salt, pepper and paprika. Melt butter in a roasting tin and put the venison in the tin and roast for 16-20 minutes.

Meanwhile, heat the game juices in a pan and add the wine. Stirring frequently, cook until the sauce is thick. Take the pan off the stove and leave the sauce to cool for a few minutes. Dice 100g butter and whisk it into the sauce, and season.

Halve the figs and heat them along with the grapes in some butter. Take the venison out of the roasting tin when it is ready and carefully remove the meat from both sides of the ribs and cut into slices about 2cm in size.

Add a little water to the roasting tin, scraping the tin with a wooden spoon to loosen the juices. Sieve the liquid straight into the sauce.

Arrange the meat on two warmed plates and garnish with the warm figs and grapes. Serve the sauce separately with pasta.

## Creamy Venison Cutlet

*4 small venison cutlets*
*flour*
*1 tbs. butter*
*pepper*
*100g mushrooms*
*500ml good red wine*
*100 ml cream*

Wash the meat, dry thoroughly and coat in a little flour. Fry briefly in very hot butter and season with salt and pepper. Take the meat out of the pan and keep it warm. Fry the mushrooms in the cooking fat and add the wine. Simmer for 5 minutes, season and add the cream. Warm the sauce and pour over the meat and serve. Serve with mashed potatoes and cooked red cabbage.

## VIRGINAL VEGETARIANS

*"There are some fruits, which may refresh, but are also a great many which make one hot, and unfortunately, it is to these that women most often reach. They reach to the various greens, which are in flower and taste good in soups and salads, such as: asparagus, artichokes, morels, truffles, and other mushrooms. Furthermore, their cooks knew how to prepare the new spices deliciously, and serve very well; these spices are also busily prescribed by doctors. After these wonderful dishes take care, you poor lovers and husbands! Can you not foresee, that your honour is done for, and you will be exchanged and deceived?"*

Pierre de Bordeille, Sieur de Brantome, French writer (1540-1614).

## Seduce me with... Spinach and Ricotta Gnocchi

*butter*
*400g leaf spinach*
*150g ricotta*
*2 eggs*
*flour*
*100g grated parmesan or pecorino cheese*
*grated nutmeg*
*pepper*

Heat 2 tbs. butter in a wide pan, and sweat the spinach over a low heat for 2 minutes, until the spinach juices have evaporated. Press the spinach over a sieve to remove excess juices. Add the ricotta. Stir in the eggs, and 80g flour and a quarter of the cheese. Season with nutmeg, salt and pepper and leave the mixture to cool for about half an hour.

Bring plenty of water to the boil. Add salt.

Coat your hands in flour, fashion the mixture into little balls. Carefully place the balls into the lightly simmering water to cook for 5-8 minutes. It is a good idea to do a test run with one gnocchi ball - if the dough does not hold together properly, add a little more flour.

Take out the gnocchi using a slotted spoon, and drain well. Put 2 tbs. melted butter in a fire-proof dish, put the gnocchi in the dish and sprinkle the rest of the cheese over the gnocchi. Finally, put some small cubes of butter over the top of the cheese and place in a preheated oven to 200°C until the cheese has melted. Serve with a salad.

*"Women who hate potatoes are frigid and uptight. Potato lovers give their lovers hours of lustful pleasure and are never ill tempered."*
Kiichi Kurijama

## Scrumptious Gnocchi with Juicy Sage Butter

*500g boiled potatoes*
*1 egg*
*80-150g flour*
*100g grated parmesan or pecorino cheese*
*for the sauce:*
*80g butter*
*12 sage leaves*
*pepper*

Cook the potatoes in their skins until they are boiled and floury in texture. While they are still warm, peel their skins off, and puree. As soon as they are a little cooler, add the egg, flour and a pinch of salt, and knead until the mixture does not stick to one's hands. Add as much flour as the potatoes need to absorb.

Roll into a sausage about the thickness of one's fingers and cut into 2-3cm long pieces. Lay each piece over a fork, press down lightly, and roll slightly - the sauce will adhere more effectively to the indentations. Bring some salted water to the boil and put the gnocchi into the water. When they float, they are done; take them out with a slotted spoon, and drain well. Put on the serving plate.

For the sauce, warm the butter, finely chop the sage leaves and add them, seasoning the butter with salt and pepper. Pour over the gnocchi and sprinkle with the cheese.

## Alluring Aubergine Parmigiana

*2 large firm aubergines*
*1/2 onion*
*1 can plum tomatoes*
*bunch of basil leaves*
*olive oil for frying*
*2 cakes buffalo mozzarella cheese*
*2 eggs*
*6 tbs. grated parmesan or pecorino cheese*

Cut the aubergines into round slices approximately 1cm thick. Rub the slices with salt and stack them on top of each other on a plate. Cover the aubergines and place a weight on the top of the stack and leave for 1-2 hours; this is so that the bitter juices can be extracted from the aubergines.

In the meantime, make the tomato sauce (which will be cooked without adding fat). Heat the tomatoes in a saucepan. Finely chop the half onion and add it to the tomatoes, along with some basil leaves. Stir occasionally, and cook until the sauce has reduced and thickened slightly. Add some salt when the sauce is cooked, and remove from the heat.

Wash the aubergine slices and pat them dry with a kitchen towel. Heat the olive oil and fry the aubergine slices a few at a time on both sides, until they are golden brown. When they are cooked, put them on a kitchen towel to absorb the excess oil.

Chop up the mozzarella and the rest of the basil leaves. Mix the eggs, salt, pepper and eight tablespoons of the tomato sauce into the basil and cheese. Lay one third of the aubergines in a fireproof dish and cover with about three tablespoons of the tomato sauce.

Next, spoon a thin layer of the mozzarella mixture over the sauce. Put another layer of aubergines on top of the sauce, and keep on layering the ingredients in the same order until there are three layers. If the aubergines on the top of the dish are not fully covered, use the rest of the tomato sauce to make sure that the aubergines are not exposed. Finally, top the sauce with grated parmesan cheese and bake in an oven pre-heated to 180°C for 45 minutes.

Serve with 'Spring-In-Your-Step' salad

*If one believes the Greek doctor, Dioskurides, carrots can entice one towards adulterous liaisons. In East Asia, carrots are served as a substitute for ginseng. In an ancient cookery book it is written: "The yellow root, the carrot, will bring lust to conjugal matters! Spiced with parsley, this lust will be heightened still more."*

## Moroccan Carrots

*1 bunch carrots*
*3 cloves garlic*
*1/2 bunch parsley*
*1-2 sprigs mint*
*pepper*
*oil*
*vinegar*
*1 tbs. ground caraway*

Peel the carrots and cut into slices about 1cm thick. Halve the cloves of garlic and boil the carrots and garlic in salted water, so that they are still slightly crunchy. Meanwhile, chop up the parsley and mint. Leave the carrots to cool and season with salt, pepper, oil and vinegar. Mix in the herbs and the caraway and serve.

*'Whoever eats a lot of asparagus, will have many lovers'*
folk saying

## Asparagus with Hollandaise Sauce

*750g white asparagus*
*sugar*
*2 tbs. butter*
*500g baby new potatoes*
*2 tbs. bread crumbs*
*150g cooked ham (optional)*
*150g smoked ham (optional)*

*for the hollandaise sauce:*
*125g cold butter*
*2 egg yolks*
*lemon juice*
*2 tbs. white wine or water*
*white pepper*
*cayenne pepper*

Wash and peel the asparagus and cut off the ends of the stalks then Leave them to stand in boiling salted water with a pinch of sugar and a little butter for no longer than 25 minutes. Remove the asparagus and wrap it in a serviette, so that the asparagus is kept warm and the excess moisture is absorbed.

Boil the potatoes in their skin for 20 minutes, or until they are ready, and then peel the skin off. Fry the breadcrumbs in melted butter until they are light brown in colour. Reserve the cooking fat to coat the potatoes in before serving.

For the sauce, finely dice the butter into small cubes. Stir the egg yolk with a little lemon juice and the wine together in a metal basin. Place the basin in a moderately warm bain-marie and beat the sauce until it is foamy. The water should not be too hot or the sauce will curdle. Gradually add the butter bit by bit and stir in thoroughly. Do not add more butter until the last amount has thoroughly melted in.

When all the butter has melted in, remove the sauce from the bain-marie and season with the cayenne pepper and black pepper, salt and some lemon juice. Serve the asparagus with both types of ham and the sauce.

*It is not only the high vitamin and mineral content of mushrooms that makes them essential to any lovers' menu. It is because they grow, like love, mysteriously in the shadow of the night, appearing as if from nowhere by morning.*

## Papardelle with Black Truffles

*1-2 black truffles (fresh or tinned)*
*75g butter*
*black pepper*
*50ml dry white wine*
*100g single cream*
*300g papardelle (wide, ribbon noodles)*

Clean the truffles and dry immediately, peel, and cut into thin strips. Heat the butter until it is foaming, and then sweat the truffles over a low heat for a few minutes and season with freshly ground black pepper and salt. Take the truffles out of the pan and set aside, add the wine and cream to the pan and cook until the sauce is thick and creamy.

In the mean time, cook the noodles until they are al dente. Mix the truffles back into the sauce and season with salt and pepper. Pour liberally over the noodles and serve immediately.

## Fennel and Wild Rice Bouquet

*2 heads fennel*
*100g wild rice*
*100g long grain rice*
*1 shallot*
*40g butter*
*2 tbs. sherry*
*pepper*
*1-2 tbs. roasted pine kernels*
*6 nasturtium flowers*

Clean the fennel and cook in salted water for 20 minutes. Add the wild rice to boiling water with a pinch of salt and after 10 minutes of cooking, add the long grain rice. Cook for a further 20 minutes.

Halve the fennel and hollow out the insides. Dice the shallot and fry in butter, along with the fennel. Add the drained rice and season with salt, pepper, sherry and the fennel leaves. Stuff the halves of the fennel and garnish with pine kernels and the nasturtiums.

## Intoxicating Braised Celery

*2 sticks celery*
*250ml white wine*
*3 tbs. chopped herbs (parsley, chervil, chives)*
*pepper*
*4 tbs. bread crumbs*
*4 tbs. soft butter*

Slice the celery into equally sized pieces. Blanch for 3 minutes in salted water. Pour the wine and herbs into a fire-proof dish. Add the celery and season with salt and pepper. Mix the bread crumbs and the butter and add to the vegetables.

Bake for 20-25 minutes in an oven that has been pre-heated to 200°C.

Variation: Instead of the bread crumbs and the butter, one can substitute roquefort cheese to spread over the celery.

## Glazed Turnip with Nuts

*500g turnip*
*2-3 tbs. walnut oil*
*pepper*
*grated nutmeg*
*3 tbs. chopped walnuts*
*5-6 tbs. stock*
*125ml whipped cream*

Remove the leaves and roots from the turnip and peel. Leave the smaller turnips intact and cut the larger ones into quarters. Fry in oil, and season with salt, pepper and nutmeg and add the nuts. Pour in the stock, and cook for 30 minutes over a low heat. Finally, add with the cream.

## Radish Country Curry

*1 large white radish (mouli) weighing approx. 400g*
*1 clove garlic*
*2 small onions*
*1 beef tomato*
*30g melted butter*
*1 tbs. curry powder*
*1/2 tsp. ground caraway*
*pepper*
*1 tsp. grated ginger*
*soy sauce*
*30g chopped cashew nuts*
*100g full fat yoghurt*
*1 tsp. lemon juice*
*1/4 bunch flat leafed parsley*

Clean the radish and cut or slice into pieces about 3cm long and 5mm wide. Chop the onion and garlic very finely. Boil the tomato, peel its skin off and chop finely.

Put the melted butter in a saucepan and fry the curry powder, pepper and caraway, taking care not to burn it, and then add the onion, garlic, and ginger, and cook for 5 minutes. Add the radish, salt, and some soy sauce and cook for a further 15 minutes. Finally, add the tomato, nuts, yoghurt and lemon juice and cook for 2 minutes. Pull the leaves off the bunch of parsley, and use them as a garnish for the curry.

## Randy Ratatouille

*4 tomatoes*
*1 yellow pepper*
*1 red pepper*
*1 small aubergine*
*2 small courgettes*
*2 medium sized onions*
*2 cloves garlic*
*3 tbs. olive oil*
*pepper*
*1-2 tbs. chopped fresh herbs (thyme, rosemary, oregano, basil, parsley)*

Remove the skins and seeds from the tomatoes and coarsely chop. Cut the rest of the vegetables into narrow strips. Chop the onions and garlic and fry them in the heated oil. Add the peppers and aubergines and fry for 10 minutes, stirring frequently. Add the tomatoes and courgettes and cook for 10 minutes without the lid, so that the ratatouille is not too liquid. Season with salt, pepper, and the chopped herbs, and finally cook for another 15 minutes before serving.

## Potato and Courgette Gratin

*400g parboiled potatoes*
*1-2 small courgettes*
*1 clove garlic*
*20g butter*
*1 onion*
*200ml cream*
*100ml veal, chicken or vegetable stock*
*pepper*
*grated nutmeg*
*40g grated emmental cheese*

Slice the zucchini into round pieces about 5mm thick. Peel the parboiled potatoes and cut into thin slices. Run an cake tin with half a clove of garlic and grease with some butter. Layer the potatoes and courgettes in the tin, overlapping each other slightly. Peel the onion, dice and fry it in butter until they are glassy in appearance. Pour in the stock and the cream and season with salt, pepper and nutmeg. Pour the onion and stock mixture over the vegetables and sprinkle the cheese on top and bake in an oven pre-heated to 150°C for 40 minutes, or until the top of the gratin is golden brown.

## Kohl Rabi in a Piquant Sauce

*2 large kohl rabi*
*1 bunch spring onions*
*1 tbs. butter*
*100ml sour cream*
*1 tsp. lemon juice*
*white pepper*
*sugar*
*grated nutmeg*

Cut the heart shaped leaves off the kohl rabi. Peel them and remove the roots. Quarter the vegetables and cut each quarter into very thin slices. Slice the spring onions in fine rings, up to the older green leaves at the top of them.

In a large pan, melt some butter and fry the kohl rabi slices for 5 minutes. Add the spring onions and cook for a short time before stirring in the cream. Season with salt, pepper, lemon juice, a pinch of sugar and the nutmeg. Cook for a few minutes over a low heat.

Garnish with the kohl rabi leaves that were removed earlier and serve with rice or boiled potatoes.

## CLIMAX!

*"A most unusual style of table decoration originated and it was, for a long time very popular in both England and France: it was a representation of the male sexual organ and the female private parts, constructed of dough and sugar. These were presented to guests at banquets, and this was undoubtedly intended to stimulate jokes and conversation..."*

R. Warner in "Antiquitates culinariae" (1791)

## Melt-in-Your-Mouth Strawberries with Wine Mousse

*200g strawberries*
*1 tbs. sugar*
*1 tsp. lemon juice*

*for the wine mousse:*
*125g cream*
*2 egg yolks*
*3 tsp. sugar*
*1/2 tsp. grated lemon rind*
*grated nutmeg*
*1 tbs. cognac*
*30g dark chocolate*

Halve the strawberries and mix in the sugar and lemon juice. Share out between two large fluted glasses and keep cook until serving. For the mousse, whisk the cream until it is stiff and then put it in the fridge. Shortly before serving, create a bain-marie by placing a high sided basin over a pan of hot water and place the following in the basin: egg yolks, sugar, lemon rind, a pinch of nutmeg and cognac. Keep the pan on a low heat and whisk the ingredients into a foam. Leave to cool for 1-2 minutes, fold in the cream serve with the strawberries, and sprinkle with grated chocolate just before serving.

## Poached Pears for Two

*500ml muscat wine*
*1/2 nutmeg*
*1/2 stick cinnamon*
*1 large bay leaf*
*1/2 lemon*
*1 tbs. finely chopped ginger*
*1 tsp. cloves*
*1 tsp. cardamom seeds*
*1 tsp. pimento seeds*
*1 vanilla pod*
*2 pears with stems*
*200ml whipping cream*
*1/2 tsp. cinnamon powder*
*1/2 tsp. vanilla extract*
*1/2 tsp. grated nutmeg (or to taste)*
*1/2 tsp. pimento*
*1/2 tsp. ground ginger*
*1/2 tsp. clove powder*
*1 tbs. sugar*
*to garnish: mint leaves*

Pour the wine into a saucepan and add the nutmeg, cinnamon, bay leaf, lemon juice, ginger, cloves, cardamom and pimento, as well as the vanilla pod, which should be sliced open. Simmer for 30 minutes. In the mean time, peel the pears. Strain the spicy liquid through a sieve. Place the pears in the liquid and cook for 10-20 minutes, or until the pears are soft. Place one pear on the centre of a large plate and spoon a little - not too much - of the juice around the pear. Leave the pears to cool.

Add the powdered spices and the sugar to the cream and whip until it is stiff. Serve with the pears and garnish with mint leaves.

## Citrus Fruits Captured in Cream Jelly

*125ml whipping cream*
*sugar*
*1 piece ginger in syrup*
*2 sheets white gelatine*
*50ml orange juice*
*20g brazil nuts*
*1 orange*
*1 blood orange*
*1 mandarin*
*to garnish: candied orange*

Whip the cream until it is almost, but not quite stiff, and stir in 1 tbs. sugar and 1 tbs. ginger syrup. Soften the gelatine in cold water for about 10 minutes and drain well. Dissolve the gelatine in the orange juice over a low heat, allow to cool a little, and then fold into the cream. Add sugar to taste.

Remove the brown skin over the nuts and chop them finely, along with the ginger. Fold both the nuts and the ginger into the cream. Fill the cream into 2 individual jelly moulds and chill them for at least 6 hours.

Peel the oranges and cut into slices. Peel the mandarin and separate into segments, removing the film that covers each segment. Empty the moulds onto a plate each and arrange the fruit attractively around the jellies.

## Sweet-As-You Banana Flan

*2 bananas*
*3 eggs*
*500ml milk*
*1 tbs. sugar*
*1/2 tsp. vanilla essence*
*1/2 tsp. grated lemon rind*
*1 tsp. butter*

Peel the bananas and cut into pieces 2-3cm long. Whisk the eggs, add the milk, and then mix in the sugar, a pinch of salt, vanilla and lemon rind. Grease a fireproof flan dish and pour in the egg mixture. Arrange the banana pieces vertically in the mixture. Cook in an oven pre-heated to 200°C. The flan should not be too firm when it is taken out. This flan can be served hot or cold.

## Plump Plums in White Wine

*400g plums*
*1 tbs. lemon juice*
*2 tbs. sugar*
*300ml white wine*

Briefly dip the plums in hot water, and peel off their skins. Halve the plums, remove the pits, and cut into pieces. Mix with lemon juice and sugar, pour the white wine over them and leave to cool for 2-3 hours.

## Exotic Rosehip Fruit Salad

*for the cream:*
*400ml milk*
*1 packet of vanilla pudding*
*1 egg (separated)*
*40g sugar*
*1 tsp. ground ginger*
*3 tbs. unsweetened rosehips (from a health food shop)*
*rind of 1 orange*
*100ml whipping cream*

*for the fruit salad:*
*2 oranges*
*100g kumquats*
*1 pomegranate*
*1 apple*
*2 tbs. orange liqueur or orange juice*

*for the sauce:*
*rind of 1 lime*
*30g sugar*
*1 packet vanilla sugar*

In a saucepan, cook a pudding using the milk, pudding powder, egg yolk, sugar and a pinch of salt. Add the ginger, the rosehips, and the orange rind. Beat the egg white into stiff peaks and fold into the pudding and leave the mixture to cool. Whip the cream until it is stiff, and then carefully cold into the cream.

For the salad, fillet the oranges, and reserve any juice that results. Wash and halve the kumquats (cut larger fruits into quarters) Halve the pomegranate and remove the seeds. Peel and core the apple and cut into pieces. In the juice that was reserved from filleting the orange and the orange liqueur, steam the fruit for 3 minutes, and then leave to cool.

For the sauce, take the grated lime rind and lime juice, and stir in the sugar and vanilla sugar. Pour over the prepared fruit and serve with the rosehip sauce.

## Up-All-Night Espresso Mousse

*3 egg whites*
*60g sugar*
*4 tbs. freshly brewed espresso*
*2 tsp. dark rum*
*1 sheet gelatine*
*125 ml whipping cream*
*coffee powder*

Whisk the egg whites into a soft foam. Take care not to over-whisk.

Stir one teaspoon of rum into the hot espresso and fold into the egg whites. Using the whisk, beat the espresso into the egg whites until the mixture cools. Soak the gelatine in cold water and dry it out well. Dissolve the gelatine into the remaining rum over a low heat. Carefully mix into the egg and espresso mixture.

Put the mixture in the fridge and leave to cool for about 20 minutes so that the mixture can set.

Whip the cream until it stands stiff, and carefully fold two thirds of the cream into the set mixture. Fill two ramekins with the espresso mousse and put them in the freezer for 15 minutes prior to serving. Just before the mousse is served, top with the rest of the cream and dust with a little coffee powder.

## Sensuous Zabaglione with Vanilla Ice Cream

*50g caster sugar*
*3 egg whites*
*150ml marsala*
*2 large scoops vanilla ice cream*

Create a bain-marie: place a high-sided basin over a pan of simmering water. Put the sugar and egg whites in the basin and whisk into a soft foam. Add the marsala and stir continuously. Stir until the mixture is foamy and has thickened.

Serve immediately in a sundae glass with a scoop of ice cream with each serving.

## Baked Banana Melange

*2 ripe bananas*
*2 tsp. lime juice*
*butter*
*2 tbs. orange juice*
*2 tsp. Caribbean dark rum*
*2 tbs. brown sugar*
*cinnamon*
*4 tbs. grated coconut*

Peel the bananas and dribble lemon juice on them immediately, to prevent the bananas from going brown. Slice the bananas lengthways and lay in a greased baking tin.

Combine the orange juice, rum and sugar and pour over the bananas. Bake in an oven pre-heated to 200°C.

## Tantalising Tiramisu

*150ml espresso or strong coffee*
*2 tbs. dark rum (or more, according to taste)*
*100g sponge fingers*
*1 tbs. cocoa powder*

*for the cream:*
*4 eggs (separated)*
*1/2 tsp. vanilla essence*
*100g caster sugar*
*300g mascarpone cheese*

Prepare the coffee and leave it to cool. Mix in the rum and set aside to cool. Beat the egg yolks, vanilla and sugar into a thick, runny cream, add the mascarpone and mix well.

Beat the egg whites until it forms stiff peaks and carefully fold into the egg yolk mixture.

Arrange half of the biscuits in the bottom of a glass serving-bowl, and moisten them with the rum. Spread half the mixture over the biscuits. Put another layer of biscuits over the cream and top the biscuits with the rest of the cream. Leave to cool in the fridge for 4-6 hours. Shortly before serving, dust the top of the tiramisu with cocoa powder.

## Hot and Cold Grapefruit

*1 large grapefruit (ruby red or yellow, according to taste)*
*3 tbs. sugar*
*2 tbs. kirsch*
*vanilla ice cream*
*1 egg yolk*
*1/2 tsp. vanilla extract*
*2 egg whites*
*1 tbs. candied fruit*
*1 tbs. icing sugar*

Halve the grapefruits. Carefully remove the grapefruit segments. It is best to use a grapefruit knife. Lay the segments in a dish and mix with 2 tbs. sugar and some kirsch. Leave to stand in the refrigerator for 1 hour.

Take the empty halves of the grapefruit and clean them well, removing any remaining fibres. Fill the halves with ice. Put the ice-filled grapefruit halves in the deep freeze.

Whisk the egg yolk, the rest of the sugar and the vanilla extract into a pale coloured cream. Separately, beat the egg whites with a pinch of salt until it stands in stiff peaks. Carefully mix the egg yolk cream, the candied fruit and the egg white foam together. Remove the grapefruit shells from the freezer and divide the fruit segments between them. Put the egg mixture in an icing tube and squeeze it over the grapefruit using a star shaped nozzle. Bake the grapefruit briefly in an oven heated to 240°C, so that the top browns, and serve immediately.

## Thrilling Coconut and Mango Cream

*25g grated coconut*
*milk*
*2 tbs. tinned coconut cream*
*2 tbs. white rum*
*2 sheets white gelatine*
*1 large egg*
*30g sugar*
*1/2 lemon or lime*
*125g whipped cream*
*1 small mango*
*100ml passion fruit juice*

Put the grated coconut in a dish and cover with warm milk, and leave to stand, so that the coconut absorbs some milk. Mix the coconut cream with the rum. Soak the gelatine in cold water for 5 minutes. Peel the zest of the lemon or lime, using a zester, and chop the ribbons into small pieces.

Beat the egg, sugar and lemon or lime zest into a thick cream. Stir in the swollen coconut and the rum mixture.

Place the gelatine in a saucepan while it is still dripping wet and dissolve over a low heat and fold into the cream. Leave the mixture to stand in the fridge until the mixture is semi-set. Then fold the whipped cream and leave the mixture to cool and set in the fridge for a further 3 hours.

Peel the mango and cut into slices.

Place the mango and the passion fruit juice in a saucepan and steam for a few minutes. Allow to cool, and then serve with the coconut cream on a plate.

## Mint and Melon Wonder

*30g mint leaves*
*1-2 tbs. honey*
*cardamom*
*3 sheets of white gelatine*
*1/3 honeydew melon*
*2 tbs. lemon juice*

*for the wine mousse:*
*1 egg*
*2 tbs. sugar*
*125ml white wine*

Put some of the mint leaves aside. Wash the rest of them and place them in a teapot with 250ml boiling water. Leave them to brew for 10 minutes, and then pass the tea through a fine sieve. Add the honey and cardamom. Soften the gelatine in cold water for about 5 minutes, drain well, and dissolve in the hot tea. Using a melon baller, cut balls out of the honeydew. Lay 6 balls aside and put the rest into the tea along with some lemon juice and the rest of the mint leaves (leave a few leaves aside to garnish). Pour into 2 individual jelly moulds and leave to set in the fridge for 6 hours.

For the sauce, combine the egg, sugar and wine in a bain-marie, and whisk into a thick foam. Turn out the jellies onto a large plate, pour over some sauce and, on the side, garnish with mint leaves and melon balls.

## THE SPRING OF LOVE

*There are many more archaic preconceptions about drinking than there are about eating - such as the belief, for example, that by drinking something, the soul of the matter drunk is immediately absorbed. Alcoholic beverages and the resulting intoxication helps to establish erotic contacts and to intensify them.*

## APERITIFS

### Adonis

*per glass:*
*30 ml sherry*
*15ml Vermouth rosso*
*15ml Vermouth bianco*
*a couple of dashes of bitter orange*

Stir all the ingredients thoroughly in a large glass over ice. Transfer the cocktail into pre-cooled cocktail glasses and serve.

### South Sea Dream

*per glass:*
*50ml coconut milk*
*2 tbs. pureed fresh pineapple*
*20ml freshly squeezed lime juice*
*10ml white rum*
*to garnish: 1/4 slice pineapple, 1 mint leaf*

Mix the ingredients with ice in a cocktail shaker and serve over crushed ice in a cocktail glass. Decorate with the pineapple slice and mint leaf.

## Red Fire

*per glass:*
*20ml orange liqueur*
*2 tbs. lemon juice*
*4 very ripe pureed strawberries*
*champagne*

Mix the ingredients well, and add the champagne, stir well and serve in a cocktail glass.

## Angel's Delight

*per glass:*
*40ml single cream*
*a couple of dashes grenadine*
*20ml triple sec*
*20ml gin*

Shake all the ingredients very vigorously in a cocktail shaker with lots of ice, and pour into cocktail glasses.

## Devil

*per glass:*
*20ml dry Vermouth*
*30ml port*
*a dash of lemon juice*
*lemon peel*

Stir the ingredients well, over ice, and transfer into pre-cooled cocktail glasses. Decorate with lemon peel.

## Knockout

*per glass:*
*20 ml dry Vermouth*
*20ml gin*
*a couple of dashes of Pernod*
*a dash of creme de menthe*

Stir the ingredients well, and transfer them to chilled martini glasses.

## Leave it to Me

*per glass:*
*20ml dry Vermouth*
*20ml gin*
*a couple of dashes lemon juice*
*a couple of dashes maraschino*
*a couple of dashes apricot brandy*

Shake in a cocktail shaker with ice and pour into a Martini glass

## Fallen Leaves

*per glass:*
*20ml Vermouth rosso*
*10ml dry Vermouth*
*20ml Calvados*
*a dash of brandy*
*lemon peel*

Stir the ingredients over a lot of ice and pour into a chilled cocktail glass. Sprinkle with lemon juice and add the peel.

## Elderberries with Champagne

*60g elderberries with the stems removed*
*125ml dry Riesling*
*100ml mineral water*
*100ml dry sekt/sparkling wine*
*juice of one lemon*
*1 clove*
*250ml champagne*
*to garnish: raspberries, wild strawberries,*
*2 sprigs lemon balm*

Wash the elderberries in a colander, shake well and leave to try on a kitchen cloth. Put into a pan all the ingredients shown in the list up to the champagne. Place the flowers in a stoneware or glass bottle and pour the warm liquid over them. Cover with a cloth and keep cool for one week. Strain the mixture through a fine sieve and freeze in a deep freezer for 2-3 hours. Keep stirring the mixture regularly, so that the crystals that form are not too big. Shortly before the sorbet completely sets, stir in 3-4 tbs. champagne and allow to fully freeze.

Scoop out the sorbet and place in a champagne balloon. Pour with champagne and decorate with berries and lemon balm.

## ALCOHOLIC DRINKS

### Persian Love Potion

*black tea*
*11/2 tbs. sugar*
*plum slices*
*rum*

Brew 500 ml black tea and leave to stand for 5 minutes, mix the sugar in and leave to cool.

Place the slices of plum in the tea glass, pour in a shot of rum and fill the glass with the cooled tea. Finally, add 2 ice cubes to each glass.

### Ginger Beer

*1 litre beer*
*1 tbs. ground ginger*
*1/2 tsp. grated nutmeg*
*3 fresh eggs*
*honey*

Mix the beer with the ginger and nutmeg in a saucepan and cook very slowly over a low heat. Meanwhile, beat the eggs, a little cold beer, and some honey with a whisk until the mixture is foamy. Pour in the heated beer. Chill before serving, although this drink can also be enjoyed hot as well.

## Spiced Coffee

*3 tbs. cocoa powder*
*2 tsp. cinnamon*
*grated nutmeg*
*3 tbs. honey*
*2 mugs hot coffee (600ml)*
*40ml rum*

Mix the cocoa, cinnamon, nutmeg and honey, adding one or two drops of water to help the ingredients mix. Stir into the coffee, and add rum to taste.

## Celery Bowl

*1 large stick celery*
*finely ground rock candy (to taste)*
*cognac (to taste)*
*2 bottles white wine*

Clean the celery and cut into thin slices. Put in a glass bottle with the sugar, and seal it so that it is airtight. Leave to stand in a cool place, and in the evening, pour in the cognac and leave to stand overnight. Before drinking, add the wine.

## Ginseng Wine

*1 long ginseng root (fresh or dried)*
*500 ml rice wine*

Pour the rice wine over the ginseng root and leave to stand for a month. Drink one glass daily. The root should stay in the wine.

## Banana Wine

*3 kg over-ripe bananas*
*50g fresh yeast*
*300g sugar*

Puree the peeled bananas. Finely grate the yeast and mix well with the sugar. Put everything in an earthenware pot, and add water and keep covered for three months. Filter the brew and serve chilled.

## Spiced Wine

*1 bottle red burgundy wine*
*30g cinnamon*
*30g ground ginger*
*10g ground cloves*
*1/2 vanilla pod*
*400g sugar*

Put all ingredients in a saucepan, cover it and leave to stand for 1 hour. Filter the wine through muslin before serving.

## Special Tequila

*handful of hemp buds*
*1 piece fresh hemp root*
*1 chilli pepper*
*700ml tequila*

Add all the ingredients including a pinch of salt to the tequila and leave to stand for a week. Serve chilled, perhaps with freshly squeezed lemon juice. Do not eat the solid ingredients.

## COCKTAILS

### Bee's Kiss

*Per glass:*
*20ml cream*
*runny honey to taste*
*30ml white rum*
*10ml brown rum*

Shake all the ingredients thoroughly in a cocktail shaker with ice and serve in a cocktail glass

### Between the Sheets

*per glass:*
*20ml lemon juice*
*10ml triple sec*
*20ml brandy*
*20ml white rum*

Put all the ingredients in a cocktail shaker along with ice and shake thoroughly. Serve in a cocktail glass.

## Pina Colada

*per glass:*
*40ml coconut milk*
*60ml pineapple juice*
*60ml white rum*

Use an electric mixer to blend all the ingredients with some crushed ice and pour into a large tumbler.

## Green Leaves

*per glass:*
*mint leaves*
*20ml creme de menthe*
*tonic water*

Put the mint leaves in a large tumbler, and pour the creme de menthe over them. Crush the mint leaves with a spoon, top with crushed ice and fill the glass with tonic water and stir.

## Coconut Lips

*per glass:*
*60ml pineapple juice*
*40ml single cream*
*10-20ml coconut cream*
*10ml raspberry liqueur*
*to garnish: maraschino cherries, pineapple.*

Shake all the ingredients thoroughly in a cocktail shaker with lots of ice. Serve over crushed ice in a large tumbler. Decorate with cherries and pineapple.

## Latin Lover

*per glass:*
*10-20ml lemon juice*
*20ml Rose's lime cordial*
*40-60ml pineapple juice*
*20ml Cachaca*
*20ml tequila*
*to garnish: pineapple*

Mix all the ingredients with crushed ice and shake well in a cocktail shaker. Serve in a large tumbler with crushed ice. Garnish with pineapple.

## Pick Me Up

*per glass:*
*10ml lemon juice*
*20-30ml brandy*
*dash of angostura bitters*
*dash of grenadine*
*a few dashes of sugar syrup*
*champagne*

Shake all the ingredients except the champagne thoroughly in a cocktail shaker with some ice. Pour into a champagne flute and top up with champagne.

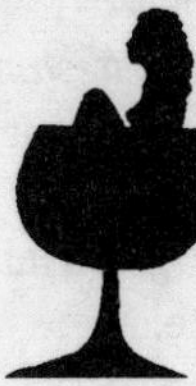

## TEA, COFFEE AND COCOA

### Fresh, Enlivening Tea

*500g fresh tea (twigs and leaves)*
*2 litres still mineral water*

Wash the tea, and put in the cold mineral water. Bring to the boil and cook on a rolling boil for 30 minutes. Fill a teapot with it. With the tea leaves, you can prepare up to three brews. The tea should be drunk unsweetened.

### Chinese Ginger Tea

*for two cups:*
*4-6 pieces ginger root*
*2 tsp. sugar*

Place the ginger in 4 cups water and boil until half the liquid is left. Add sugar, and drink the tea while it is hot.

### Moroccan Peppermint Tea

*1/2 sprig fresh mint*
*sugar or honey*

Put the mint leaves in a glass and pour in boiling water. Sweeten according to taste.

## Ginseng Tea

*1 tbs. ginseng root*
*1 tbs. ginger root*
*1 tbs. liquorice*
*1 date*
*honey or sugar*

Bring all the ingredients to the boil and leave to stand. Strain the tea and sweeten with honey or sugar. Drink once daily for aphrodisiac effect.

## Vietnamese Sweet Talking Tea

*1 litre still mineral water*
*2 sticks sugarcane*
*5 sticks liquorice*
*2 mint sprigs*
*1 tsp. black tea*

Bring the water to the boil. Chop up the sugar cane and liquorice. Wash and dry the mint sprigs. Place all the ingredients in a teapot and pour in the boiling water. Brew for 5 minutes.

## Cardamom Coffee

*1 heaped tsp. ground filter coffee*
*1 heaped tsp. cardamom seeds*
*honey or sugar*
*milk*

Mix the coffee and the cardamom seeds and brew in boiling water. Sweeten according to taste and add milk.

## Pineapple Tea

*6 tsp. black tea*
*1 fresh pineapple, cut into slices*
*juice of one lemon*
*750ml still mineral water*
*finely chopped candied ginger*

Brew the tea for 5 minutes and leave to go cold. Slice four slices of pineapple and squeeze lemon juice on them. Add the tea to the pineapple and chill. Before serving, add the mineral water and the ginger.

## Mexican Cocoa

*1 litre milk*
*2 vanilla pods*
*4 tbs. cocoa*
*2 tbs. honey*
*4 tbs. sugar*
*chilli*

Slowly heat the milk on a low heat with the vanilla pods. After 10 minutes, remove the vanilla, slit the pods open and scrape out the core. Mix the seeds with the cocoa and 250ml water and pour into the hot milk. Add the honey and sugar, along with a pinch of chilli powder and salt. Take the pan from the stove and whisk the cocoa until it is foamy.

## Iced Tea with Ginger

*12 tsp. black tea*
*1 litre still mineral water*
*brown sugar*
*1 lemon*
*pickled ginger*

Brew the tea for 5 minutes, using the mineral water. Fill tall glasses two thirds full with ice cubes and pour the tea over them. Sweeten according to taste with brown sugar. Decorate the glasses with lemon slices and sliced ginger.

## Anti-stress Cocoa

*5 heaped tsp. cocoa*
*1-2 tsp. cinnamon*
*1-2 knife tips cardamom powder*
*1 knife tip clove powder*
*1/2 vanilla bean pod*
*1 pinch chilli (according to taste)*
*4-6 tsp. honey*

Bring all the ingredients to the boil in 500ml water and boil for 5 minutes.

## MISCELLANEOUS DRINKS

### Celery Water

*1 tsp. celery seeds*

Leave the celery seeds to stand in two glasses of water for 8 hours. Strain the seeds out and drink daily.

### Guarana Drink

*guarana seeds*
*1 litre boiling water*

Crush a handful of guarana seeds in a pestle and mortar and add to the water. After 5-10 minutes, strain out the seeds and drink. The seeds can be used four times to make tea.

## Honey Water

*1 sprig rosemary*
*1 sprig sage*
*1 sprig rue*
*watercress*
*250g fresh honey*

Place the herbs in a glass filled with honey and leave for three months, taking care to seal the glass. To prepare the drink, brew 1 tsp. honey in boiling water and drink regularly.

## Krishna's Drink

*2 cups almonds*
*2 cups blueberries*
*2-4 tbs. maple syrup (according to taste)*

Soak the almonds overnight. The next day, put the almonds in boiling water for 11/2 minutes. Remove the brown skin and chop the nuts. Slowly add 4 cups of water. Puree the blueberries through a sieve and into the almonds. Sweeten with maple syrup.

## OBJECTS OF DESIRE - MENUS FOR LOVERS

*Babette Hersant knows how to cook - and it is written to that effect in the recommendation she carries with her on a stormy September night in 1871. She steers a boat to the Jutland coast, to a little village of low houses and stooped gables: the 35-year old is fleeing.*
*In France it is the Civil War, and her husband and son have already been slaughtered. A friend sent her to this sparce tip of Denmark, recommending her services to the two sisters Martine and Philipa. Neither of them are young, and they are both quite puritanical, inspired by ascetic love for humanity as a whole. Their father was a priest, philosopher but he has been dead for years. Now the sisters care for the old people of the village, continuing his work. What else is there to do on God's earth! Babette wants to stay with them, despite the eternally grey clouds, the obstinate grass, and the plain fare: bread soup with a shot of beer and a fish stew, which never, ever varied.*

*For fourteen years, Babette bowed to this diet, observed people becoming old, who in spite of the eternal psalm-singing, started slowly to rake up the sins of their youth: little jealousies, deceptions, amorous escapades, and all just before the most important celebration, the centenary of their communities' religious faith.*

*Just before the anniversary, a letter arrives from Paris - Babette has won 10,000 Francs in the lottery. Will she return to France? She does. But only for one week, to shop for the jubilee feast, which she will prepare. And in all of this, she only has one wish - a french dinner!*
*She brings with her chirping quails, a gasping turtle, innumerable boxes and baskets and a whole block of ice. Amazed, the community watches the disembarkation of these exotic things. What are her intentions? The sisters are plagued by nightmares of hissing*

*monsters and intoxicated witches, fearing that on their day of honour, vice will lead them into temptation because they are threatened by a witch's sabbath! But there is no turning back.*
*Babette covered the long table with white linen and discreetly decorated it with feathers and flowers. Candles burning, reflecting in the precious porcelain and the many different glasses at each setting. In the kitchen the helpers are busy, plucking quails, skinning the calf's head, slaughtering the turtle, baking pasties, unwrapping bottles of wine from the protective straw. Humming, Babette pours the soup to the croutons into the cups. At last, serving starts.*

*After an 'Amontillado', the General, an unexpected guest from Paris, states with surprise, this is the best he has ever had. Enter the turtle soup! A feast for the palate. "Only one glass each", Babette reminds her helper, and sends him in with a bottle of Veuve Clicquot, year 1860. With that she serves "Blinis Davidoff". Oysters, garnished in black and white. "Red wine goes into the large glasses", explains Babette, as she decorates the beheaded quails, stuffed with truffles in pastry cases, with snails and herbs. The guests respond with some irritation to the arrival of the tiny birds. 'How is one to eat these? Ah, that's how the General does it, bites into the crunchy-crisp head of a quail and sucks noisily the brain out?!' The General casts his mind way back, when he tasted these "Cailles en sarcophage" for the first time in the Cafe Anglais in Paris: "The chef was, surprisingly, a woman. She had the rare gift of transforming each meal into a love affair, into an affair between the physical and spiritual appetite. She was the greatest culinary genius on earth!" He sips some red wine and in amazement he registers its quality - a Clos de Vougeot 1845.*

*Slowly, the care-worn faces around the table lighten up into blissful smiles. The diners chatter, remembering beautiful moments of the past. Salad is served in small bowls, and still more red wine flows.*

*Large pieces of cheese for dessert, and the rarest of fruits: figs, papayas and grapes. The feast is never-ending. Still more food - a cake decorated with cherries and blossoms, with coffee, freshly ground, of course. A small glass of Vieu Marc de Champagne before returning home - and they fall into each other's arms: "Let us sing and kiss to brotherhood!" Forgotten are the rivalries of old, all are laughing, and are happy as rarely before: the stars had suddenly moved closer together.*

**Scene from the film "Babette's Feast" by Gabrielle Axel.**

## SPRING FEELINGS

**Asparagus Salad**

•

**Tempestuous Turbot in a Riesling Cream Sauce**

•

**Rhubarb and Strawberry Fool**

## Asparagus Salad

*150g green beans*
*50g fresh button mushrooms*
*pepper*
*1 tbs. lemon juice*
*50g carrots*
*200g freshly cooked asparagus*
*2 tbs. cold pressed virgin olive oil*

Cook the beans in salted water for 5-7 minutes, pour the hot water out and wash in cold water so that the beans keep their colour. Clean the mushrooms, and cut into thin slices, and season with salt, pepper and lemon juice. Peel the carrots and cut into long fine strips. Cut the asparagus into pieces approx. 4cm long and halve the beans. Combine the carrots, mushrooms and beans, and place the mixture next to the asparagus on the plate and drizzle with olive oil.

## Tempestuous Turbot in a Riesling Cream Sauce

*2 turbot (each weighing approx. 200g)*
*lemon juice*
*2 shallots*
*1/2 bunch shallots*
*100g cold butter*
*100ml dry white wine (Riesling)*
*1 large beef tomato*
*80g button mushrooms*
*100ml single cream*
*pepper*
*creme fraiche*

Wash the fish in cold water, dab dry and season with lemon juice. Finely chop the shallots and chervil. Take 30g butter, melt it in a pan and fry the shallots until they are translucent in colour, and then add the fish fillets. Add the chervil, wine and 3 tbs. water and steam with the lid on the pan for 13 minutes.

Meanwhile, remove the skin and seeds from the tomato and cut into slices. Clean the mushrooms and slice. Take the fish out the pan and keep warm. Pour the cream into the cooking juices, and bring to the boil. Add the tomato and mushrooms and keep warm. Dice the cold butter and using a whisk, beat in the butter a little at a time until the sauce is thick and creamy. Season with salt and pepper, and add the creme fraiche. Pour the sauce over the fish and garnish with a few chervil leaves. Serve with tagliatelle.

## Rhubarb and Strawberry Fool

*400g rhubarb*
*100g sugar*
*2 sheets white gelatine*
*100g strawberries*
*icing sugar*
*1 egg white*
*125ml whipping cream*
*2 sprigs mint*

Peel the rhubarb, and cut the stalks into small pieces. Place them in a saucepan and sprinkle 80g sugar over the rhubarb. Leave to stand for 2 hours. After the fruit has stood, cook it until it is so soft that it has turned to a mush.

Soak the gelatine in cold water for 5 minutes, drain well and dissolve it in the rhubarb compote. Leave to cool, until the mixture is gelatinous. Meanwhile clean and halve the strawberries, except for two, which still have their stems and are attractive enough to use as a garnish. Dust the strawberries with icing sugar.

Beat the egg white until it stands in stiff peaks and mix the rest of the sugar into the egg white. Beat the cream until it is stiff and fold carefully into the rhubarb mousse. Mix in the strawberry halves. Fill the mixture into two tall glasses and garnish with the whole strawberries and the mint leaves.

## SUMMER HEAT

**Gazpacho**

•

**Pampered Pigeon and Peas**

•

**Vanilla Ice Cream with a Flambéd Strawberry Sauce**

## Gazpacho

*1 small unpickled gherkin (200g)*
*1 fully ripe tomato*
*1 red pepper*
*1 egg yolk*
*2 tbs. olive oil*
*1 tbs. sunflower oil*
*1 tsp. red wine vinegar*
*pepper*
*1 small slice white pepper*
*1 clove garlic*

Peel, halve and de-seed the gherkin. Boil the tomato briefly, remove its skin, halve it, and remove the seeds. Cut out the pepper core, discard it and cut the flesh in half. Finely dice a quarter of the vegetables and puree the rest of them in a blender. Beat the egg yolk, 1 tbs. olive oil, sunflower oil and vinegar until it is a thick cream. Add the vegetable puree and season with salt and pepper, and leave to cool in the fridge for 1-2 hours.

Finely dice the white bread. Heat 1 tbs. olive oil in a pan and fry the garlic until it is golden brown. Remove the garlic and then fry the bread to make garlic croutons. Serve the soup in two bowls and garnish with the diced vegetables and croutons.

## Pampered Pigeon and Peas

*2 young pigeons*
*pepper*
*2 slices streaky bacon*
*1 tbs. melted butter*

*For the stuffing:*
*1/2 bread roll*
*75ml poultry stock*
*100g chicken liver*
*30g lean bacon*
*1 tbs. butter*
*1 large shallot*
*1 tsp. chopped parsley*
*1 tbs. chopped herbs (basil, thyme, marjoram)*
*1 tsp. chopped pistachios*
*1 egg*

*For the sauce:*
*1 shallot*
*1 tsp. butter*
*100ml Madeira*
*200ml poultry juices*

Prepare the pigeons for cooking: remove the neck and wings and loosen the skin from the neck and over the breast. Wash the birds and dry well.

For the stuffing, finely chop the bread roll, pour the stock over the bread and leave to soak in. Squeeze out excess liquid from the bread. Remove the liver and hearts of the birds, and halve them, and chop up the chicken liver. Finely dice the bacon and the shallot. Fry the liver and giblets, the bacon and the shallots in butter. Add the parsley and some of the herbs and fry for a little longer. Take half of the mixture and mix with the bread roll and puree. Mix the egg, pistachios and the rest of the herbs with the remaining giblet mixture.

Season the insides of the pigeons with salt and pepper and fill the abdominal cavities with the stuffing, and also in the loosened skin over the breasts. Place the slice of bacon over each bird, and using kitchen string, sew the bird up so that the stuffing is secured and the bacon is fixed to the pigeon breast. Fry the birds in hot butter until they are golden brown, turning them frequently. Remove the pigeons and keep warm and pour out excess fat from the pan, and add 4 tbs. water to the remaining cooking juices to make the sauce.

For the sauce, chop up the pigeon wings and the shallot and fry them in butter, and douse frequently with the Madeira, so that a jus is created. Strain the sauce through a sieve and season with salt and pepper and add the rest of the herbs.

Remove and discard the bacon from the pigeons, and place the birds on the plates. Pour the sauce over them and serve with side dishes of peas and duchess potatoes

## Duchess potatoes

*200g well-boiled potatoes*
*1 egg*
*grated nutmeg*
*2 tsp. butter*
*1 egg yolk*
*1 tbs. cream*

Boil the peeled potatoes in salted water until they are soft, and then place them in a baking tin and let them dry out in a hot oven for a few minutes - all the moisture from boiling must be evaporated. Mash the potatoes and work in the egg, nutmeg and salt. Stir in 1 tbs. butter.

Smear a baking tray with butter. Spoon the potato into an icing tube, with a large star-shaped nozzle and squeeze out potato rosettes onto the tray. Mix the egg yolk and the cream and brush onto the tops of the rosettes. Bake the potatoes in a preheated oven until the tops of the potatoes are golden in colour.

## Vanilla Ice Cream with a Flambéd Raspberry Sauce

*200g raspberries*
*1 tbs. lemon juice*
*2 tbs. sugar*
*1 tbs. raspberry jam*
*2 tbs. raspberry liqueur*
*2 portions vanilla ice cream*

Mix the raspberries with lemon juice, sugar, and raspberry jam. Warm the mixture over a low heat and at the end add the raspberry alcohol. Once the sauce is warm enough, flambé, until the alcohol has burnt off, and then serve over the ice cream.

## AUTUMNAL LONGINGS

**Snails in Herb Sauce**

•

**Wild Mushroom Consommé**

•

**Make-Me-Swoon Venison Medallions with Mashed Celery**

•

**Cheese Plate**

### Snails in Herb Sauce

*butter*
*1 tbs. cream*
*1 tbs. white wine*
*1 clove garlic*
*1 tsp. finely chopped cloves*
*1 tbs. mixed herbs (chervil, tarragon, thyme, rosemary)*
*pepper*
*1 piece toast*
*1 tomato*
*12 tinned snails, without their shells*

Mix 1 tbs. of the butter with the cream, wine, crushed garlic and herbs and set aside.

Very finely dice the slice of toast and fry in some butter to make croutons. Place the tomato in boiling water for a few minutes, peel off the skin and then halve the tomato, remove the seeds and finely dice. Salt the tomato and then fry it lightly in some butter. Heat the snails in the juice from the tin and then drain them well.

Fill 2 ramekins with the snails and garnish with the diced tomato and croutons. Serve hot with a baguette.

## Wild Mushroom Consommé

*25g dried wild mushrooms*
*500ml veal stock*
*1 small egg white*
*75g fresh wild mushrooms*
*1 tbs. oil*
*black pepper*
*2 tbs. rubbed chives*

Wash the dried mushrooms in hot water and then leave them to soak in the lukewarm stock. Lightly beat the egg white and stir into the stock. Bring the stock to the boil and leave covered for 15 minutes.

Line a sieve with muslin and sieve the stock, without stirring or pressing it through; the stock should be crystal clear. Clean the fresh mushrooms and cut them into slices. Fry them briefly in hot oil and season with salt and pepper.

Place the mushroom slices in pre-warmed bowls. Season the consommé, reheat it without allowing it to boil and pour over them and garnish with chives. Serve with fresh bread.

## Make-Me-Swoon Venison Medallions

*4 venison medallions (about 3cm thick)*
*grated ginger*
*black pepper*
*1 small carrot*
*1 small onion*
*1 tbs. oil*
*20g butter*
*250ml game stock*
*2 tbs. double cream*

Rub the meat with the ginger, salt and pepper and keep cold. Peel the onion and carrot and finely dice them. Heat the oil and butter in a pan, and fry the medallions over a medium heat for 2-3 minutes on each side. The meat should still be juicy on the inside. Remove the meat and wrap it in aluminium foil and leave to stand. Sweat the carrot and onions in the fat from frying the meat, pour in the stock and reduce the mixture to half the original volume. Purée the sauce and strain it through a sieve back into the pan, and stir in the double cream. Cook the sauce briefly and season with a pinch of sugar, salt and pepper. Arrange the meat on the plates and pour any juices from the meat into the sauce. Serve the sauce separately, along with a side dish of mashed celery.

## Mashed Celery

*250g celery*
*2 tbs. double cream*
*1 tbs. burnt butter*
*1 tbs. whipped cream*

Peel the celery and cut into small pieces. Cook the celery in salted water until it is soft. Pour off the water and add the double cream and then puree the celery with a potato masher. Mix in the butter and season with salt. Before serving, fold in the whipped cream.

## WINTER STORMS

**Marinated King Prawns**
•
**Beef Fillet Fanfare**
•
**Apple and Potato Gratin**
•
**Baked Apples with Custard**

### Marinated King Prawns

*2 limes*
*2 oranges*
*sugar*
*1 small red onion*
*1 red chilli*
*1 small beef tomato*
*1 bunch flat parsley*
*fresh coriander*
*8 green king prawns*

Wash the fruits and grate the rinds. Juice all 4 fruit and mix the juice and rind together in a large bowl. Season with some salt and the sugar and mix well.

Peel the onion and cut into wafer thin rings and add them to the juice. Remove the chilli seeds and discard, and chop the chilli very finely and add them to the bowl.

Boil the tomato for a few minutes and remove its skin, halve it and discard the seeds. Finely dice the flesh and add to the marinade.

Bring some salted water to the boil and add the prawns and

place them in the boiling water. Leave them to cook in the covered pan on a low heat for about 4 minutes. Pour out the water and rinse the prawns in cold water to stop them from cooking. Leaving the tails on, remove the shells an carefully remove the vein with a toothpick. If desired, the prawns can be cut lengthways in half before swirling them through the marinade.

Serve on a bed of salad, with a little marinade poured over the prawns.

## Beef Fillet Fanfare

*2 fillets of beef (each weighing 100g)*
*black pepper*
*200g chicken liver*
*1 tbs. raisins*
*2 tbs. cognac*
*2 tbs. finely chopped shallots*
*butter*
*100ml stock*
*2 tbs. Madeira*
*1 bay leaf*
*thyme*
*pepper*
*1 tsp. tomato puree*
*1/2 tsp. meat stock cube*
*cayenne pepper*

Wash the fillets in cold water and dry thoroughly. Rub the meat with coarsely ground black pepper. Cut the chicken livers into thin slices. Wash the raisins and leave them to soak in the cognac. Sweat the onions for 2-3 minutes in 1/2 tbs. butter. Add the stock and cook over a high heat. Stir in the Madeira and add the bay leaf and reduce the liquid to half its volume slowly over a low heat. Flash fry the fillets in hot butter to seal them and set aside on a warmed plate, having seasoned them with salt.

Heat 1/2 tbs. butter in the same pan and fry the liver for a minute or two. Remove the pan from the stove and season with salt, pepper and thyme.

Add the raisins and cognac to the cooking juices and stir in the tomato purée, crumbled stock cube and the cooking juices from the steaks. Bring up to a boil for a moment, and then remove from the heat and add about 40g butter, beating it into the sauce until it melts. Season the sauce with salt, a pinch of cayenne pepper and thyme. Mix the liver into the sauce and pour over the two steaks on the serving plates.

Serve with Apple and Potato Gratin.

## Apple and Potato Gratin

*200g boiled potatoes*
*2 small cooking apples*
*1 tsp. butter*
*pepper*
*10 sage leaves*
*100ml whipped cream*
*2 tbs. olive oil*

Peel the potatoes and apples and remove the apple cores. Slice the potatoes and apples very finely and place them in layers into a greased pyrex dish. Season with salt and pepper and sprinkle coarsely chopped sage leaves on the top of the dish. Mix the cream and oil together and spread over the top. Bake in an oven pre-heated to 225°C and cook for a further 20 minutes.

## Baked Apples with Custard

*2 medium sized apples*
*1 tbs. marzipan*
*1 tsp. chopped almonds*
*1 tbs. chopped pistachios*
*1 tbs. rum*
*10g butter*
*125ml medium white wine*

*For the sauce:*
*1/2 vanilla bean pod*
*40g sugar*
*5 tbs. milk*
*5 tbs. cream*
*1 egg yolk*
*1 egg*

Remove the seeds from the vanilla pod and add them to a saucepan, along with 20g sugar to the milk and cream. Bring to the mixture slowly to the boil, stirring often. Using a whisk, beat the egg yolk, the egg and the rest of the sugar until a foamy mixture is formed. Place the hot milk into a bain-marie, and then gradually beat in the egg mixture, until the sauce thickens. Take care that the water bath does not become too hot, or the sauce will curdle. Put the sauce in a cool place.

Remove the apple cores, using an apple corer, so that the apples still look neat. Mix the marzipan, rum, almonds and half the pistachios together. Lay the apples in an oven proof dish and fill the holes where the core was with the mixture. Lay small flecks of butter on top of the apples so they do not dry out during baking. Bake in an oven pre-heated to 180°C, occasionally basting the apples with the wine.

Arrange the two apples on the plate, pour over the vanilla sauce and garnish with the remaining pistachios.

## EXOTIC LOVE MENU

**Happy Rolls**
•
**Avocado Soup**
•
**Vietnamese Coconut Rice**
•
**Burmese Chicken Curry**
•
**Tropical Fruit Salad**

## Happy Rolls

*1 egg*
*100g very lean pork (throat)*
*4 sheets rice paper*
*2 medium sized scampi*
*50g fresh soya bean sprouts*
*1/4 fresh salad gherkin*
*head of lettuce*
*1/2 bunch chives*
*1/2 bunch mint*
*1/2 bunch coriander*
*125ml Hoi Sin sauce*
*1 tbs chopped peanuts*
*1/2 bunch chives*

Beat the egg, cook an omelette and leave to go cold. Cook the pork for 15 minutes and cut into wafer thin pieces. Meanwhile, moisten the rice paper with a spray gun and lay on a damp cloth. Cook the scampi in their shell, remove the shell and halve them lengthways.

Wash the bean sprouts. Cut the gherkin into thin slices, separate the salad leaves. Cut the omelette into strips.

Put four salad leaves on the serving plates and fill with the following ingredients: pork, bean sprouts, 1/2 scampi, gherkin slices, omelette strips, chives, mint and coriander. Season with a pinch of salt.

## Avocado Soup

*1 ripe avocado*
*1 cup creme fraiche*
*1 small onion*
*2 cloves garlic*
*1 tsp. tabasco sauce*
*pepper*
*500ml hot chicken stock*
*1 tbs. fresh dill (or other fresh herbs)*

Open the avocado, remove the meat and mash it finely with a fork. Add the creme fraiche and mix it iin well. Finely chop the onion and crush the garlic cloves and mix thoroughly into the puree. Season with salt, pepper and tabasco. Pour in the chicken stock and simmer over a low heat for 15 minutes. Before serving, garnish with dill.

## Vietnamese Rice in Coconut Milk

*200g long grained rice*
*2 coconuts (400ml coconut milk)*
*5 cloves*
*1/2 stick cinnamon*

Wash the rice in cold water and drain dry. Cover with 250ml water and bring to the boil. Stir in the coconut milk and a large pinch of salt in the rice. Cook covered for another 3 minutes. Then cook over a high heat for 2 minutes so that a lot of excess moisture evaporates. Making sure that the spices are distributed evenly throughout the rice, add the cloves and cinnamon and cook on a low heat for a further 20 minutes. Take the saucepan off the heat, carefully stir the rice and keep covered for 15 minutes. Before serving, remove the spices.

## Burmese Chicken Curry

*1 small chicken or chicken pieces*
*1/4 tsp. saffron*
*1 tbs. soy sauce*
*2 tbs. curry powder*
*2 onions*
*3 cloves garlic*
*1/2 tsp. chilli powder*
*oil*
*3 bay leaves*
*1 tsp. cinnamon*

Divide the chicken into portions. Mix the saffron, soy sauce and curry together and rub into the chicken. Set aside. Finely grate the chilli, onion and garlic. In a saucepan heat the oil and fry the onion mixture. Add the chicken and fry. Add the bay leaves, cinnamon and 21/2 cups water season with salt and simmer for approximately one hour.

## Tropical Fruit Salad

*According to taste add:*
*lychees*
*fresh pineapple*
*banana*
*papaya*
*mangoes*
*star fruit*
*1 tbs runny honey*
*2 tbs grated coconut*

Prepare the fruit and sprinkle with a pinch of salt. Mix with the honey and garnish with the coconut.

# INDEX

## Index

# Index